Art of Database Management

SQL to Scale

Imran Shahid Shaikh

Copyright © <2024> <Imran Shahid Shaikh>

Made with ❤ on the Notion Press Platform

www.notionpress.com

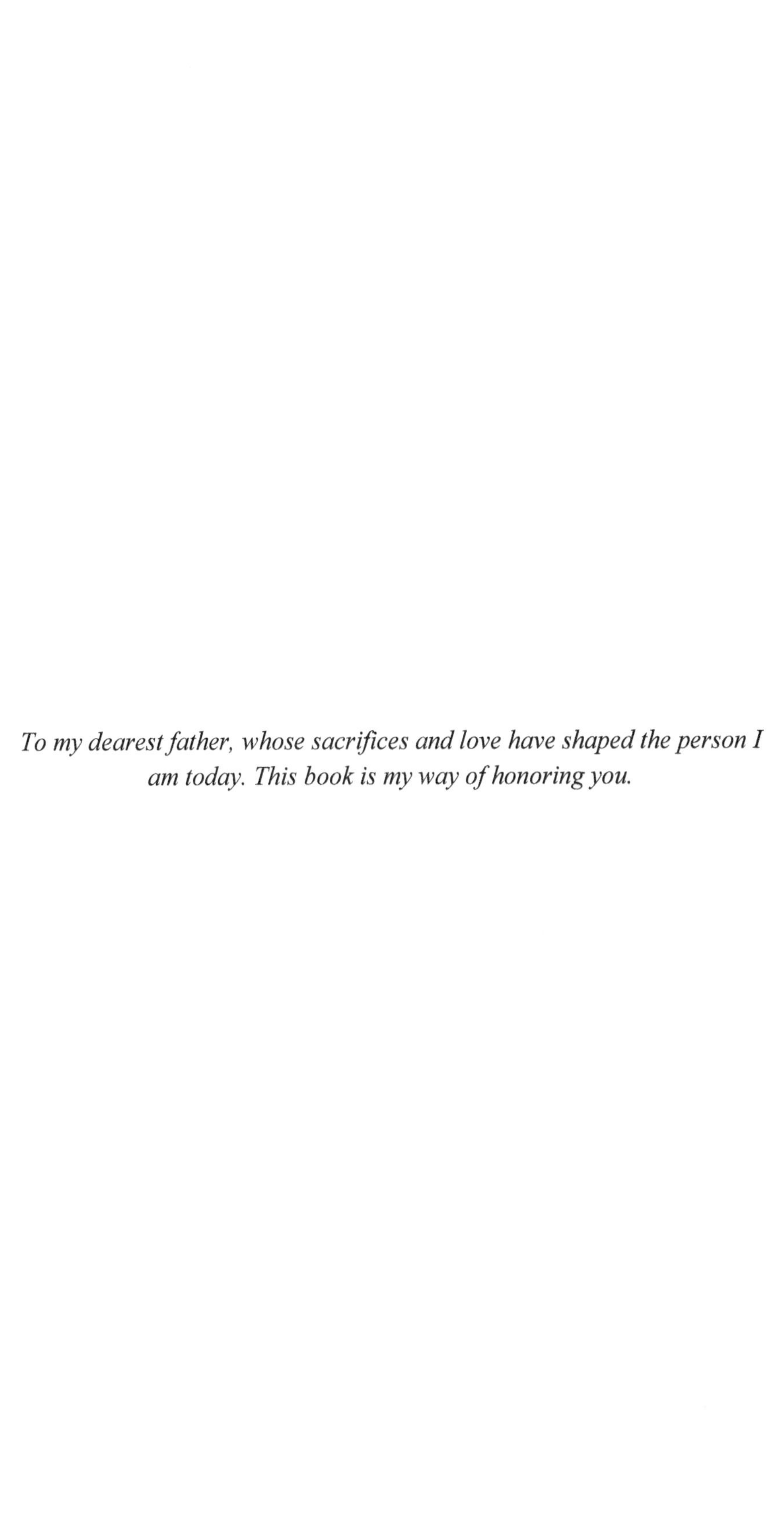

To my dearest father, whose sacrifices and love have shaped the person I am today. This book is my way of honoring you.

Contents

Preface

The idea for this book emerged from my experiences as an educator and practitioner in the field of database management. Over the years, I have witnessed students and professionals alike struggle with bridging the gap between theoretical knowledge and practical application. This inspired me to create a resource that not only explains the fundamental principles of database management systems but also demonstrates their implementation using SQL.

This book is intended for a wide audience—students pursuing computer science, professionals working with data, and anyone interested in mastering the art of database management. By combining theory with hands-on practice, my aim is to help readers build a strong foundation and gain practical skills that they can apply immediately.

The book is structured into three main sections: the first four chapters explores the theoretical underpinnings of DBMS, including topics such as relational databases, normalization, and data modelling. The chapter 5 provides a step-by-step guide to SQL, complete with examples and exercises that reinforce learning and the chapter 6 explores the concept transaction management.

I owe a debt of gratitude to my mentors, colleagues, and students who have shared their insights and feedback, shaping the content of this book. Special thanks to my family for their unwavering support during this journey.

I hope that this book serves as a valuable guide, inspiring curiosity and confidence as you delve into the fascinating world of database management systems.

Imran Shahid Shaikh

Acknowledgments

Writing this book has been a journey filled with challenges, growth, and countless moments of learning. I am deeply grateful to all those who have supported and encouraged me throughout this process.

First and foremost, I extend my heartfelt thanks to my college time professors, whose expertise, guidance, and insights have been invaluable in shaping this work.

I am also indebted to my colleagues and peers, for their thoughtful discussions and valuable input, which enriched the content and clarity of this book.

Special thanks to my students, whose questions and enthusiasm for learning motivated me to explore and explain concepts in a clear and practical manner. Your curiosity has been a constant source of inspiration.

To my family, thank you for your unwavering support, patience, and love. Your belief in me gave me the strength to complete this project.

This book is the result of collective effort, and I am deeply grateful to everyone who played a part in making it a reality. Thank you for your support and contributions.

Sincerely,

Imran Shahid Shaikh

Sr. Lecturer

AI-ARKP New Mumbai

1. Introduction to Database System

You can start typing out or copy-pasting the first chapter of your book here.

The heading style 'Heading 1' can be used from the Quick Styles gallery for the chapter heading.

As with all other chapters, the first paragraph is given a flush left alignment. This style can be chosen from the Quick Styles gallery with the name 'Normal_without indent.' All subsequent chapters have a slight indent and this style can also be availed from the Quick Styles gallery with the name 'Normal_indent.'

If you wish to insert a citation and reference as a footnote in a page, you can do so by placing the cursor where the citation number should be inserted and choosing 'Insert Footnote' from the References tab. This would add a citation number where the cursor is placed and a footnote in the same page. You can enter the reference text by clicking in the footnote.[1]

Database Concepts

Data

Data is the raw material that can be processed for any real life object for example Employee name, product name, student name student address etc.

Database

Database can be defined as organized collection of related data. Database typically shows the relations and activities of organization entities. For example an organization college management may contain entities as student, Lecturer, classroom, laboratories and so on -which are related to each other, Database for a college management system will describe

- Activities related to Students, Lecturers, Laboratories and Classrooms.

- Relationship among the Students, Lecturers, Laboratories and Classrooms.

Database Management System (DBMS)

As we already defined Database is an organized repository or collection of related data but the question arise as an alone how the user can manage Database?

Therefore, user needs a tool to manage the Database.

Database Management System or DBMS can be defined as software system that allows the user to maintain- to define, to update and to delete the database and provide controlled access to the database.

Or

Database Management System or DBMS is a collection of Database and the programs to maintain database.

History

The initial general purpose DBMS, designed by Charles Bachman in the early 1960s, was called the Integrated Data Store. It formed the basis for the network data model, which was standardized by the Conference on Data Systems Languages (CODASYL) and strongly influenced database systems through the 1960s.

In the late 1960s, IBM developed the Information Management System (IMS) DBMS, used even today in many major installations. IMS formed the basis for an alternative data representation framework called the hierarchical data model.

In 1970, Edgar Codd, at IBM's San Jose Research Laboratory, projected a new data representation framework called the relational data model. This proved to be a defining moment in the development of database systems.

File System a traditional approach

DBMS introduced somehow in early 1960s, question arises "how data stored in prior to 1960"? Answer is operating system files.

File Processing System (FPS) is the system, which provides base for storing and organizing operating system files that contains data.

If there is FPS then why DBMS comes into picture, to understand this one consider a scenario:

An educational organization has a large collection (say, 1000 GB) of data on students, employees, departments, fees collection, and so on. Several students and employees access this data concurrently. Query about the data must be answered immediately, changes made to the data by different users must be applied consistently, and access to certain parts of the data (e.g., fees data, salaries) must be restricted.

When organization use File Processing System or FPS in above scenario some drawbacks may be faced e.g.

- o Data is separated in different files. (Data Isolation)

- o Duplication of data or Data Redundancy (various files may contains same fields of data)

- o Common fields (say- Phone number) for one student or employee in different files may contain different values, which leads to loss of data consistency.

- o Difficulty in representing data from the user point of view. (also called as Difficulty in accessing data)

- o Security Issue: File Processing Systems provide only a password mechanism for security. This is not sufficiently stiff to enforce security policies in which different users (e.g. Students, Employees) have permission to access different subsets of the data.

- o File systems are not suitable to handle concurrent access on data. (Concurrent-access anomalies)

Advantages of DBMS

Data Independence

The DBMS provides an abstract view of the data that hides details such as, how data is stored, how it is represented. Abstraction of such kind provides an advantage of Data Independence.

Easy Access to Data

DBMS provide many useful utility commands or techniques that are used to retrieve data as per user need in a efficient way.

Data Integrity

Data Integrity can be defined as overall accuracy, completeness, and consistency of data. DBMS provide a high level of Data Integrity by enforcing integrity constraints on data. (We will discuss later Integrity Constraints).

Centralized Management

In FPS, data scattered in various files, and files may be in different formats, writing new application programs to retrieve the appropriate data from different files is difficult.

DBMS provides an easy way to join different relations (tables), so that we can extract required data from different relations in an easy manner.

Atomicity

In many applications, it is crucial that, if a failure occurs, the data be restored to the consistent state that existed prior to the failure. It is difficult to ensure atomicity in a conventional file-processing system.

DBMS provides transaction control utilities such as savepoint, rollback and commit to achieve the atomicity.

Security

Not all users have access permission to all type of data, but enforcing such restrictions in FPS is difficult. DBMS provides grant and revoke commands to restrict the access of a user over the data objects as well as control the behavior of them means how the user is accessing data.

Structure of a DBMS

Disk Storage

Data Dictionary

The descriptive information is itself stored in a collection of special tables called the catalog tables. The catalog tables are also called the data dictionary. We can conclude that schema of a table is stored in data dictionary (as another table). DDL (Data Definition Language) commands deal with Data Dictionary.

Data

Data denotes actual data records that a user want to store. DML (Data Manipulation Language) commands deal with Data Files.

Index Files

To speedup data records extraction process as per requirements, the user creates Indices. Indices are created on single column or on collection of columns having repeated values; Such Indices are also stored as database object in Index Files component.

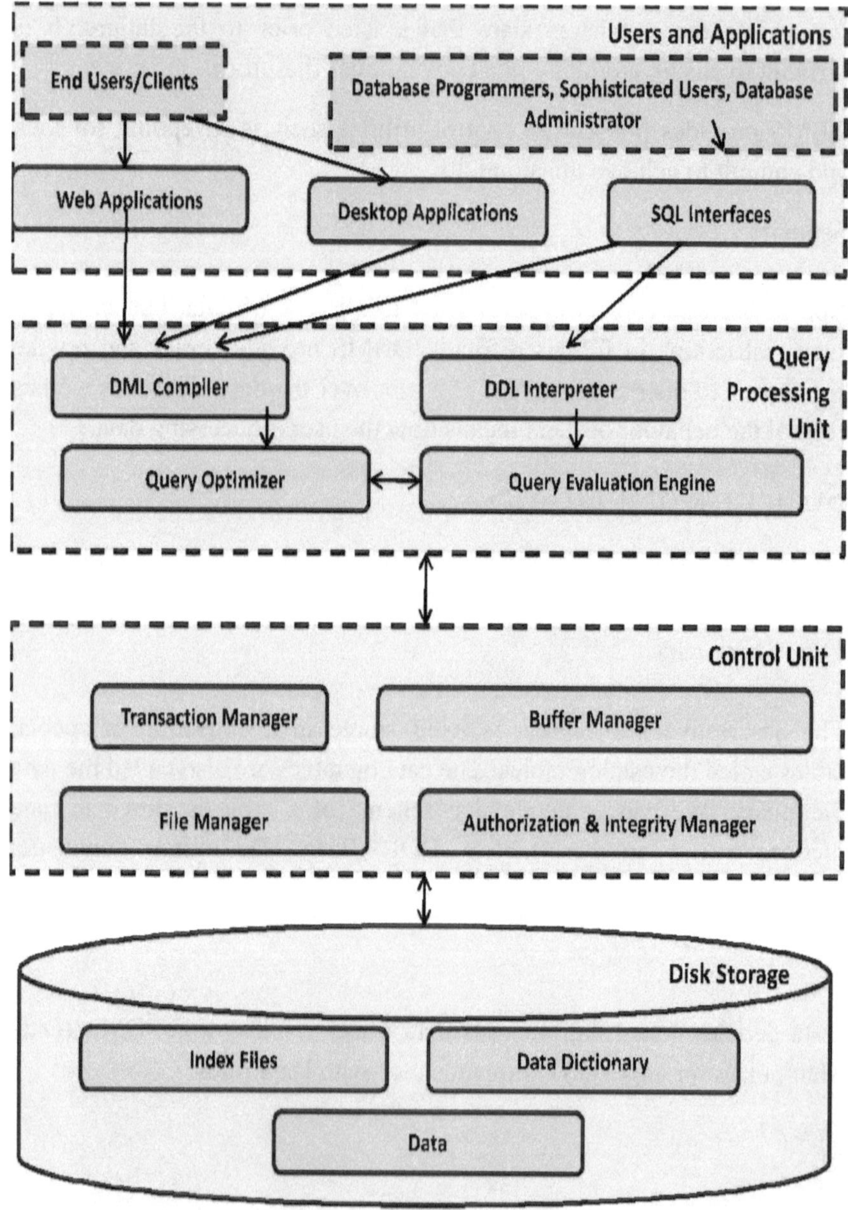

Fig. 1.1 Structure of DBMS

Storage Control Unit

Storage Control unit is responsible to manage disk storage as well as to control execution of commands. To accomplish these tasks different components are there as follows.

Authorization & Integrity Manager

This component is used to checks the user authorization to execute a command as well as checks commands against integrity constraints. Data base administrator but implementation apply integrity constraints and verification is done here. Commands that beyond user authorization or violates integrity constraints are not permitted to change the disk storage.

File Manager

File Manager responsible for the structure of the files and managing the file space. It also responsible for locating the block containing the required record, requesting this block from the disk manager, and transmitting the required record to the disk storage.

Buffer Manager

Data records are stored in data blocks at disk storage and requested by user, So Buffer manager is responsible to reads data from disk storage (hard disk) into main memory (RAM) whenever needed.

It decides which data to be cached in main memory.

Transaction Manager

The transaction manager of a DBMS controls the execution of transactions. Concurrent executions of transactions must be handle in such a way that locks must be acquired (and released at some later time) on data objects. Transaction manager ensures transaction atomicity and durability.

Query Processing Unit

DML Compiler

It translates the DML statements into low level instruction (machine language-understandable at physical level), so that they can be executed.

DDL Interpreter

It interprets DDL statements, then processes the DDL statements into a set of table containing Meta Data (data about data).

Query Optimizer

It is a process in which multiple query execution plan for satisfying a query are examined and most efficient query plan is satisfied for execution.

Database catalog stores the execution plans and then optimizer passes the lowest cost plan for execution.

Query Evaluation Engine

Responsible to execute a query plan which is selected by Query Optimizer.

Database Users

Naive users

Invoke one of the permanent application programs that have been written previously. E.g. people accessing database over the web, bank tellers, and clerical staff.

Application programmers

Interact with system through DML calls. Responsible to write application programs using DML commands.

Sophisticated users

Form requests in a database query language. Responsible to search required data from database (Data Mining).

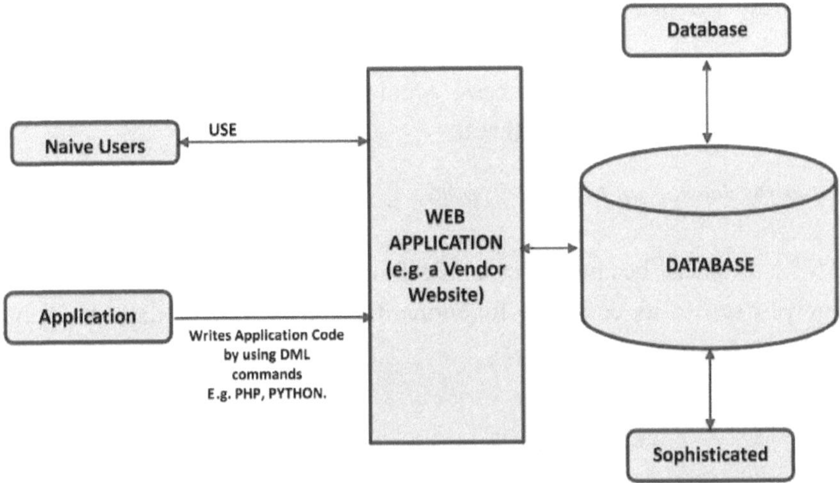

Fig. 1.2 Database Users

DBA Responsibilities

Definition of the schema

The architecture of the three levels of the data abstraction, data independence.

Modification of the defined schema

As and when required.

Creating new user

Creating new user ID and password etc., and also creating the access permissions that each user can or cannot enjoy. DBA is responsible to create user roles.

Defining the integrity constraints

It is mandatory for the database to ensure that the data entered must conform to some rules, thereby increasing the reliability of data.

Creating a security mechanism

To prevent unauthorized access, accidental or intentional handling of data that can cause security threat.

Creating backup and recovery policy.

This is essential because in case of a failure the database must be able to revive itself to its complete functionality with no loss of data, as if the failure has never occurred.

Data Abstraction

Hiding Database Design complexities from users (which are not computer professionals) is nothing but known as Data Abstraction.

- o Data Abstraction feature provide easy way to retrieve data, from database.

- o There are three levels of abstraction.

Physical level Abstraction

- o Hiding the detail about "how the data is stored actually and where it is stored in database" from user is known as physical level abstraction.

- o The physical level describes complex low-level data structures in detail.

Logical level Abstraction

- o Hiding the detail about "what data are stored in the database, and what relationships exist among those data" from user is known as logical level abstraction.

o The logical level describes simple data structures in detail.

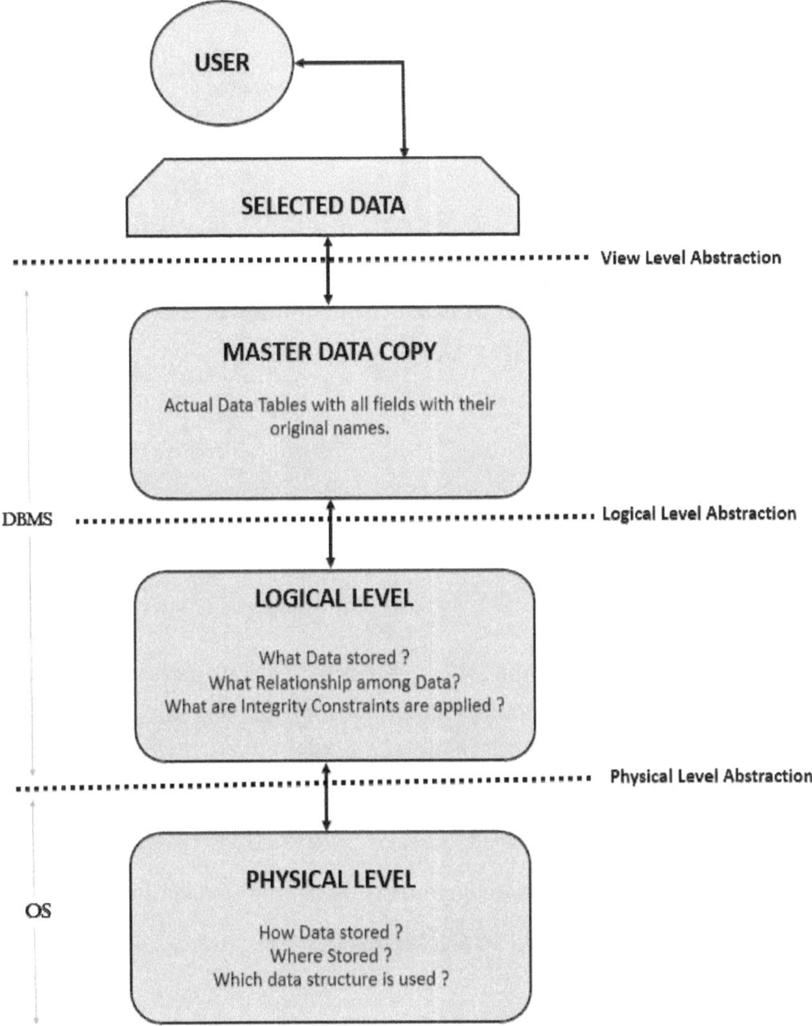

Fig. 1.3 Levels of Database Abstraction

View level Abstraction

o The view level of abstraction exists to simplify their interaction with the system. The system may provide many views for the same database, may they need to access only a part of the database.

- o Views can also hide information (e.g., salary in emp table) for security purposes.

DBMS Applications

Education

Universities and schools use DBMS for managing student records, course registration, exam results, attendance tracking, and library management. The system allows administrators to easily access and update student data.

Example:

Student information systems, course management, and library catalogs.

Banking

DBMS is used for managing customer information, transaction records, loan and credit details, and payment history. It ensures data integrity, security, and quick access to financial records.

Example

Customer account management, real-time transaction processing, ATM data, and online banking systems.

Healthcare

DBMS is critical in hospitals and clinics for maintaining patient records, medical histories, lab reports, and treatment schedules. It enables quick access to patient data for doctors and staff, helping in efficient treatment and management of health services.

Example

Electronic medical records (EMRs), appointment scheduling, and hospital management systems.

Sales

DBMS system allows the data to be stored in electronic format by making use of relational databases, which allows the data to be stored in highly organised manner. This database allows the information such as information about the customers, products, sales, purchases etc to be stored in database.

Manufacturing

DBMS is used in manufacturing for managing production schedules, supply chain data, inventory, and quality control processes. It helps in efficient resource allocation, inventory management, and process optimization.

Example

ERP systems, production tracking, and inventory management systems.

Airlines

Airlines use DBMS to manage flight schedules, reservations, customer information, and ticketing systems. The system helps optimize resources, manage flights, and provide real-time updates on seat availability.

Example

Booking management, passenger details, and flight operations.

Telecommunications

Telecom companies use DBMS to store and manage call records, customer profiles, billing information, and service subscriptions. The system helps with managing billing systems, customer support, and network management.

Example

Customer data management, billing, and prepaid/postpaid account records.

2. Overview of Database Design

Data Model

Before implementing the database through a database programming language, database is created on paper by Database Administrators, It represents relationships among the data as well as restrictions that to be followed for accepting valid data. To represent data, data relationships and restrictions on data some tools are used collection of such tools is a Data Model.

There are different types of data models among that we are considering the most popular ER Data Model.

E.R. Data Model

Graphical representation of database with all its data entities, relationships and constraints (restrictions that to be applied while accepting or deleting a data).

Entity

A real time thing or object is an entity for example consider a college database that contains real time objects such as Student, Teacher, Subject and Grade.

It is often useful to identify a collection of similar entities. Such a collection is called an entity set.

In ER Data model Entity is denoted by rectangle e.g. as follows

Subject	Teacher	Student	Grade

Relationships

As we said database is collection of related data, data entities must be associated to each other. Association between data entities is a relationship.

For example, "teacher TAUGHT a subject". In this example, there is a relationship between teacher and subject i.e. TAUGHT.

Relationships in ER Data Model are represented using diamond symbol. E.g. as follows.

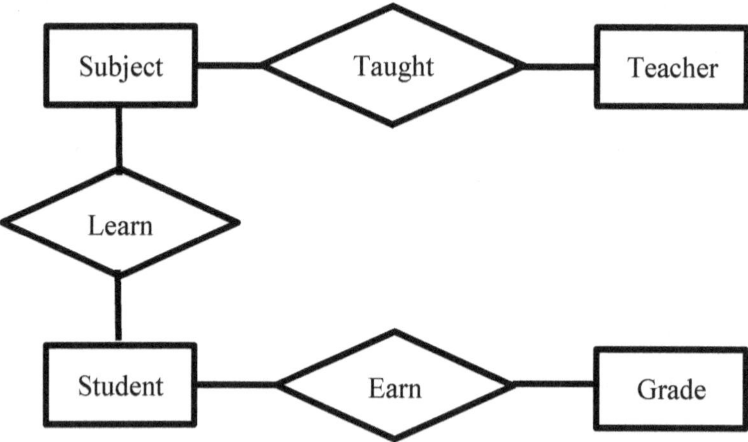

Fig. 2.1 Student-Subject-Teacher-Grade ER Diagram

Attribute

An entity is described using a set of attributes. All entities in a given entity

set have the same attributes; this is what we mean by similar. For example, a entity teacher can be described by attributes – teacher_name, teacher_qualification, teacher_dept, teaher_subject.

For each attribute associated with an entity set, we must identify a domain of possible values. For example, the domain associated with the attribute teacher_name of teacher might be the set of alphabates.

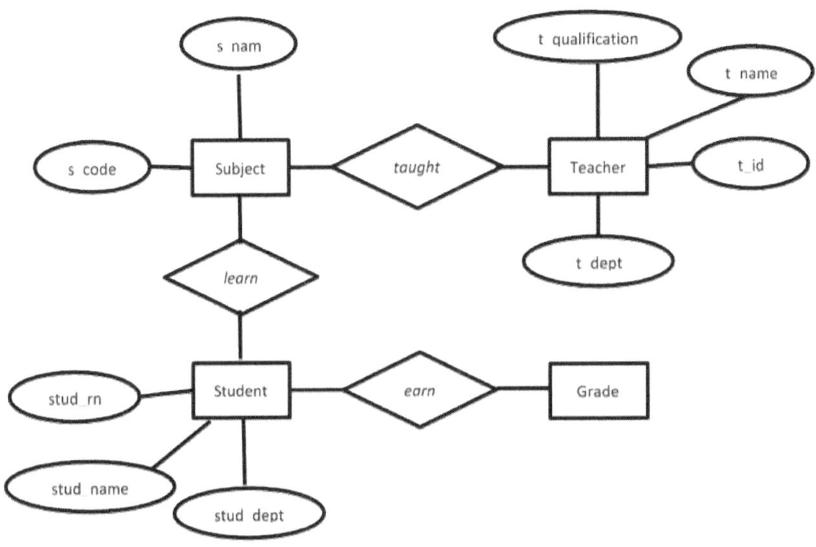

Fig. 2.2 Student-Subject-Teacher-Grade ER Diagram

Attribute Types

Simple Attribute

Attribute that cannot be further divided, not derived from any another attribute and does not have multiple values are known as simple attribute. Represented as ellipse.

Primary Key Attribute

Primary key attribute are those attributes have clearly different value for each record of an entity e.g. t_id, stud_rn and s_id have unique values for every record in that entity.

Represented as underlined ellipse.

Multivalued Attribute

Attribute those have multiple values for the record e.g. t_qualification for a teacher. One Teacher may have multiple qualifications.

Derived Attribute

Attribute those derived from another attributes e.g. gross_salary attribute can be derived from basic_salary.

or

Age attribute can be derived from date_of_birth.

Composite Attribute

This attribute can be further divided into more number of attribute e.g., t_name attribute can be divided into t_first_name, t_last_name.

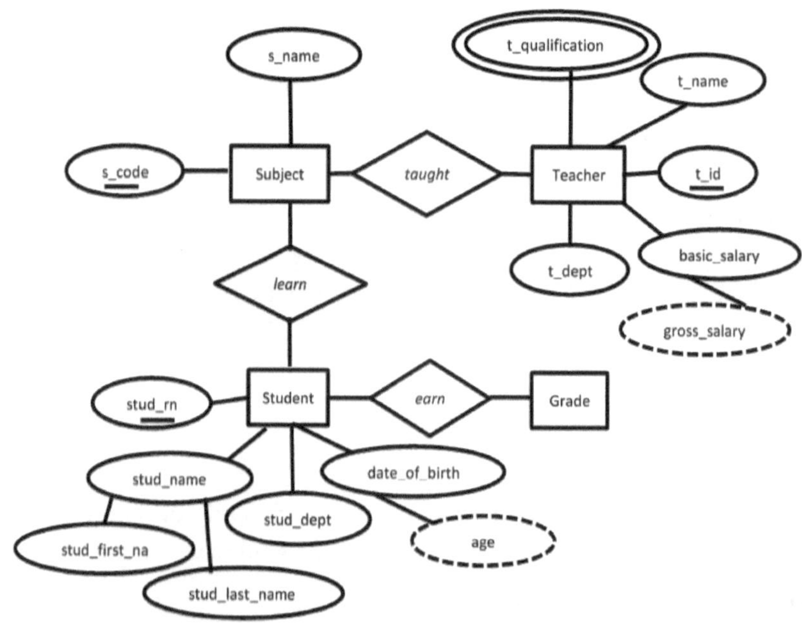

Fig. 2.3 Student-Subject-Teacher-Grade ER Diagram

Strong Entities, Weak Entities

Strong Entity

An entity set that has a primary key is termed a strong entity set.

E.g. in our example student entity have sufficient attribute to form a primary key that is s_rn, by the use of s_rn we can identify any student record uniquely.

Weak Entity

An entity set may not have sufficient attributes to form a primary key. Such an entity set is termed a weak entity set.

For a weak entity set to be meaningful, it must be associated with another entity set, called the identifying or owner entity set.

In our example if the student entity is not in the database, the grade entity will not be. There is no existence of grade entity without student entity.

So student entity will be an owner entity or strong entity that identify Grade entity.

Finally ER diagram looks like as shown in figure . with a weak entity symbol i.e. double rectangle.

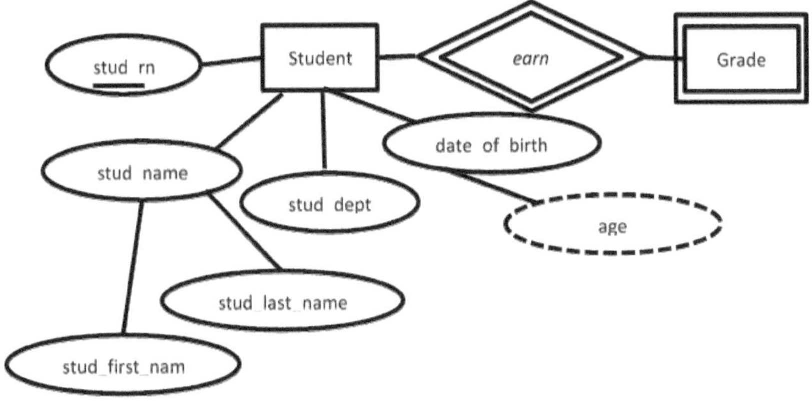

Fig. 2.4 Student-Subject-Teacher-Grade ER Diagram

Cardinality

In database, cardinality refers to the relationship among the relations, which specifies number of instances available for a relation 1 instance, in another relation 2.

For example, relation Teacher have an instance with name 'Aman',

Relationship with cardinality between Teacher Aman and Subject can be defined as

"Aman taught 3 subjects"

Here 3 is the cardinality. Therefore, we can conclude that

Number of tuples available in a relation for an instance of another relation.

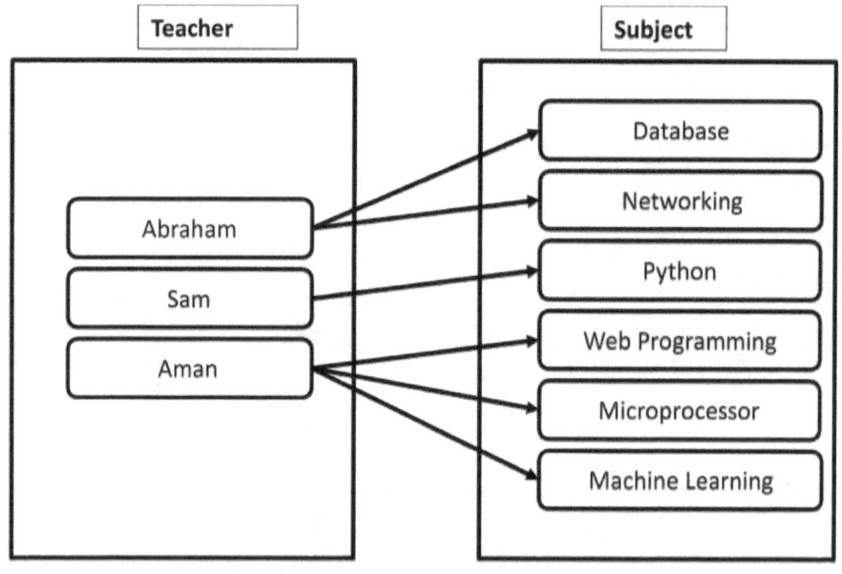

Fig. 2.5 Cardinality

Cardinality Types

- One to One

    Relation between a PERSON and PANCARD

"One PERSON can have only one PANCARD".

o   One to Many

Relationship between a TEACHER and SUBJECT

"One TEACHER can taught many SUBJECTS".

o   Many to Many

Relationship between TEACHER and STUDENT.

"Many TEACHERS taught many STUDENTS".

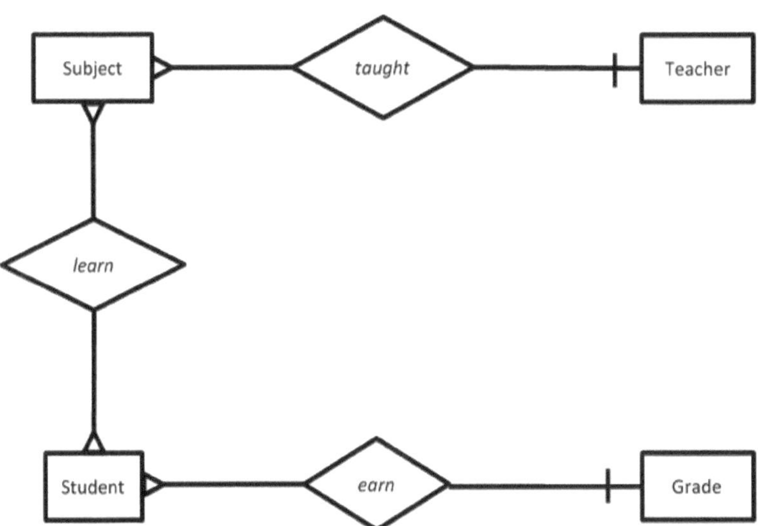

Fig. 2.6 Cardinality types

Generalization, Specialization, Aggregation

Generalization

Generalization consists of identifying some common characteristics of a collection of entity sets and creating a new entity set that contains entities possessing these common characteristics.

Typically, the subclasses are defined first, the superclass is defined next, and any relationship sets that involve the superclass are then defined.

Specialization

Specialization is the process of identifying subsets of an entity set (the superclass) that share some distinguishing characteristic.

Typically, the superclass is defined first, the subclasses are defined next and subclass-specific attributes and relationship sets are then added.

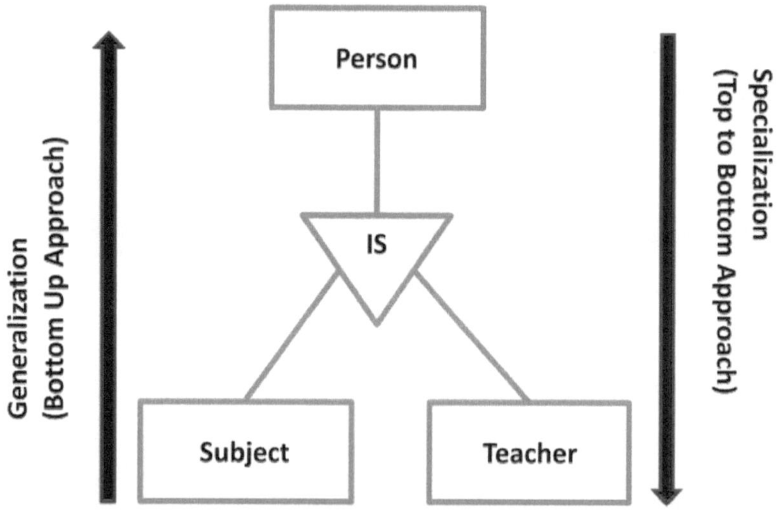

Fig. 2.7 Generalization & Specialization

Aggregation

Aggregation is a process of establishing a relationship between a relationship and an entity.

Let us consider an example of a course center, if a visitor visits a coaching center then he will never enquiry about the Course only or just about the Center instead he will ask the enquiry about both.

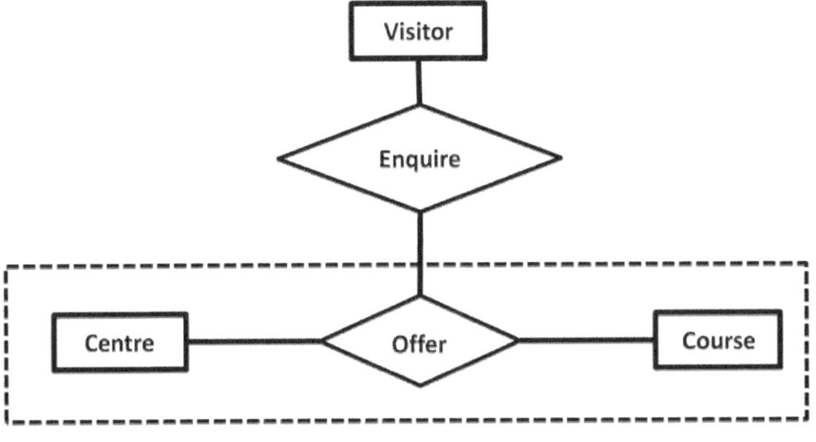

Abstract Entity

Aggregation can be summarize as

- o Treat relationship as an abstract entity
- o Allows relationships between relationships
- o Abstraction of relationship into new entity

3. Relational Model

Relational Data Model Concepts

The Relational Data Model is the foundation of relational databases, which are widely used for storing, managing, and querying structured data. It was introduced by Edgar F. Codd in 1970 and is based on the concept of organizing data into tables (or relations) and using mathematical principles (specifically, set theory and predicate logic) to manage that data.

Below are the key concepts of relational data model concepts.

Relation (Table)

A relation is a table consisting of rows and columns. Each table represents a specific entity or type of data. For example, a "Customers" table might store information about customers.

Tuple (Row)

A tuple is a single row in a table. Each tuple represents a unique record in the relation. For example, in a "Customers" table, each row might represent a single customer.

Attribute (Column)

An attribute is a column in a table that represents a specific property of the relation. For example, in a "Customers" table, the attributes might include "CustomerID," "Name," and "Email."

Domain

A domain is the set of permissible values for a given attribute. For example, if an attribute represents a date, its domain might consist of all valid dates.

Relation Schema

The relation schema defines the structure of a relation, specifying its attributes and their data types. For example, a schema might define that the "Customers" table has the attributes "CustomerID" (an integer), "Name" (a string), and "Email" (a string).

Relation Instance

A relation instance refers to the actual content of a relation at a specific point in time. It is the current set of tuples in a table.

Concept of Keys

In DBMS (Database Management System), a key is a crucial concept that helps in identifying unique rows or records within a table. Different types of keys serve various purposes, such as ensuring data integrity, maintaining relationships between tables, and optimizing search operations. Let's explore each type of key in detail with examples.

Super Key

A super key is a set of one or more attributes (columns) that can uniquely identify a row in a table. It may contain extra attributes that are not necessary for unique identification.

To understand the concept of Keys consider above relation (table).

CUSTOMER (C_ID, C_NAME, C_STREET, C_AADHAR_NO)

Superkeys in an entity set CUSTOMER

{C_ID},

{C_AADHAR_NO}

{C_ID, C_NAME},

{C_ID, C_STREET}

{C_ID, C_AADHAR_NO}

Superkey may contain extraneous attributes.

For example C_ID and C_AADHAR_NO alone can identify uniquely tuple in a relation.

{C_ID, C_NAME} superkey have a C_NAME attribute as extra attribute.

{C_ID, C_STREET} superkey have a C_STREET attribute as extra attribute.

Candidate Key

A candidate key is a minimal super key. It is the smallest set of attributes that can uniquely identify a row. A table can have more than one candidate key.

{C_ID},

{C_AADHAR_NO}

{C_ID} is a candidate key because it's a minimal super key that uniquely identifies each customer.

{ C_AADHAR_NO } is a candidate key because it's a minimal super key that uniquely identifies each customer.

So, the table could have two candidate keys: {C_ID} and {C_AADHAR_NO}.

Primary Key

A primary key is one of the candidate keys chosen by the database designer to uniquely identify rows in the table. It cannot contain NULL values, and there can only be one primary key for each table.

{C_ID}, **→ chosen, so it will become a primary key**

{C_AADHAR_NO}

If C_ID is selected as the primary key, then {C_ID} becomes the primary key, ensuring that each customer has a unique C_ID and that this field is never NULL.

Foreign Key

A foreign key is an attribute (or a set of attributes) in one table that is used to establish a relationship between two tables. It references the primary key of another table. Foreign keys help maintain referential integrity between tables.

Example:

Consider two tables:

Department(Dept_ID, Dept_Name)

Employee(Emp_ID, Name, Dept_ID)

In the Employee table, Dept_ID is a foreign key that references the Dept_ID column in the

Dept_ID in the Employee table is a foreign key that ensures that an employee must belong to an existing department.

Unique Key

A unique key is similar to a primary key in that it uniquely identifies rows, but it allows NULL values (though only one NULL value is allowed in the case of a unique key). Unlike the primary key, a table can have more than one unique key.

Example:

> In the Customer table, if we want to ensure that no two customer have the same C_AADHAR_NO but allow customers to leave the C_AADHAR_NO field empty for some reason, we can make C_AADHAR_NO a unique key.

Composite Key

A composite key is a key that consists of two or more attributes that together uniquely identify a row. It is used when a single attribute is not enough to uniquely identify a record.

Example:

> Consider a table Course_Registration(Student_ID, Course_ID, Semester)

> In this case, neither Student_ID nor Course_ID alone can uniquely identify a row, but the combination of Student_ID and Course_ID forms a composite key that can uniquely identify each row.

Relational Integrity Constraints

These are rules to ensure the accuracy and consistency of data. Key types of integrity constraints include:

Domain Integrity Constraints:

Restrict the values of an attribute (e.g., age must be between 0 and 100).

Key constraints:

Ensure that the primary key is unique and not null.

Referential integrity:

Ensures that a foreign key correctly references a valid primary key in another table.

Domain Integrity Constraints

Data Type Constraints:

Specifies the type of data that a column can hold, such as integer, character, date, etc.

Example:

A JoiningDate column in an Employee table is set to the DATE data type, ensuring only valid date values are allowed.

Length Constraints

Limits the number of characters or digits a value can have.

Example:

A PhoneNumber column is defined with a length constraint of 10 characters, meaning only values with exactly 10 characters are permitted.

NULL Constraints

Specifies whether a column can contain NULL values.

Example:

An Email column in a Users table might be set to NOT NULL, indicating every user must have an email address.

Default Constraints

Assigns a default value to a column if no value is provided during data entry.

Example:

A Status column in an Orders table can have a default value of 'Pending'. If an order is inserted without specifying the status, it automatically gets the value 'Pending'.

Check Constraints

Ensures that all values in a column satisfy a specific condition.

Example:

A Salary column in an Employees table can have a check constraint CHECK (Salary > 0) to ensure no negative salaries are entered.

Enumeration Constraints

Restricts a column to accept only a predefined set of values.

Example:

A Gender column can have an enumeration constraint to accept only 'Male', 'Female', or 'Other'.

Key Constraints

Primary Key Constraint

As we know, primary key is an attribute in a relation that uniquely identifies instances/ records in a relation. Now the question is arise what restrictions are on that attribute, if it is defined as primary key. So following are the restrictions on attribute if it is defined as primary key.

1. Uniqueness: No two rows can have the same value for a primary key attribute.

2. NOT NULL: Every record must have a value for the primary key attribute(s).

Unique Key Constraint

Ensures that all values in a column or a set of columns are unique across the table. Unlike a primary key, a unique key can contain NULL values, but each non-NULL value must be unique.

In a User's table, Email can be a unique key because each email address must be unique, though it might be NULL for some records.

	Uniqueness	NOT NULL
Primary Key	It is must	It is must
Unique Key	It is must	It may be

Table 3.1   Difference between Primary Key and Unique Key

Referential integrity

Foreign key constraint

Foreign Key establishes a relationship between the two tables, foreign key in one-table points to a primary key in another table. It ensures referential integrity, meaning that a value in the foreign key column must exist in the referenced table.

Foreign key constraint restrict a delete operation on a foreign key column in child table if there is a reference is available in parent table.

Trainer_id	Course_id

Course_id	Course_name	Course_hours

Table 3.2 Trainer-Course   *Table 3.3 Course*

If the trainer is conducting a training on a specific course (identified by couse_id in a Trainer-Course table) that course can't be deleted from Course table.

Relational Algebra Operations

Relational Algebra is a procedural query language used to query and manipulate data in relational databases. It provides a set of operations that take one or more relations (tables) as input and produce a new relation as output. These operations are fundamental to understanding how SQL queries work under the hood.

Below are the key relational algebra operations

1. SELECT (σ)

2. PROJECT (π)

3. UNION ($\cup$)

4. INTERSECTION ($\cap$)

5. SET DIFFERENCE ($-$)

6. CARTESIAN PRODUCT ($\times$)

Selection (σ)

It filters rows based on a given condition.

Syntax:

σ condition (Relation)

Example:

If we have a Students table with attributes StudentID, Name, and Age, the query

σ Age > 20 (Students)

Selects all students older than 20.

Projection (π)

Selects specific columns from a table, removing duplicate values in the result.

Syntax:

π attribute1,attribute2 (Relation)

Example:

If we have a Students table with attributes StudentID, Name, and Age, the query

π Name, Age (Students)

Will return only the Name and Age columns from the Students table.

Union (∪)

Combines the result sets of two relations, removing duplicates.

Syntax:

(π common attribute Relation1)

∪

(π common_attribute Relation2)

Example:

If we have two tables Loan and Account with a common attribute customer-name, the query Loan ∪ Account will list "all unique customer names from both tables". The relational algebra query will be as follows.

(π customer-name Loan)

∪

(π customer-name Account)

Result of above query will be a list of all customer names those either having an account in a bank or they have taken loan from a bank.

Intersection (∩)

Returns rows that are present in both relations.

Syntax:

(π common attribute Relation1)

∩

(π common_attribute Relation2)

Example:

If we have two tables Loan and Account with a common attribute customer-name, the query Loan ∩ Account will list "all common customer names from both tables". The relational algebra query will be as follows.

(π customer-name Loan)

∩

(π customer-name Account)

Result of above query will be a list of all customer names those having an account in a bank as well as they have taken loan too from a bank.

Set Difference (−)

Returns the rows present in the first relation but not in the second.

Syntax:

(π common attribute Relation1)

−

(π common_attribute Relation2)

Example1:

If we have two tables Loan and Account with a common attribute customer-name, the query Loan − Account will list "all customer names from Loan table those are not present in Account table". The relational algebra query will be as follows.

(π customer-name Loan)

−

(π customer-name Account)

Result of above query will be a list of all customer names those have taken loan from a bank but they don't have account in a bank.

Example2:

If we have two tables Loan and Account with a common attribute customer-name, the query Account − Loan will list "all customer names from Account table those are not present in Loan table". The relational algebra query will be as follows.

(π customer-name Account)

−

(π customer-name Loan)

Result of above query will be a list of all customer names those have account in a bank but they don't borrowed any loan.

Cartesian Product ($\times$)

Combines every row of the first relation with every row of the second relation.

Syntax: **Relation1 $\times$ Relation2**

Example: If Students has 3 rows and Courses has 2 rows,

Students $\times$ Courses will result in $3 \times 2 = 6$ rows.

Student_id	Student_name
1	Aman
2	Sameer
3	Rohit

Table 3.4   Student

Course_id	Course_name
101	Math
102	Physics

Table 3.5   Course

Student_id	Student_name	Course_id	Course_name
1	Aman	101	Math
2	Sameer	101	Math
3	Rohit	101	Math
1	Aman	102	Physics
2	Sameer	102	Physics
3	Rohit	102	Physics

Table 3.6   Student $\times$ Course

Relational Calculus

Relational Calculus is a non-procedural query language in database management systems (DBMS) that focuses on what to retrieve rather than how to retrieve it. Unlike relational algebra, which uses specific operations to get results, relational calculus specifies the conditions a result set must satisfy, and the system figures out how to execute it.

There are two types of relational calculus:

1. Tuple Relational Calculus

2. Domain Relational Calculus

Tuple Relational Calculus (TRC)

In Tuple Relational Calculus, the query specifies the desired tuples by describing conditions they must satisfy.

It uses tuple variables to represent each tuple in a relation and a condition to select certain tuples.

The syntax of a TRC expression is:

{ T | P(T) }

Where:

- o T is a tuple variable.

- o P(T) is a condition (predicate) that must be true for the tuple T to be included in the result.

We will use a sample relation called Employee with the following schema to understand Tuple Relational Calculus with examples.

Employee(Emp_ID, Name, Age, Department, Salary)

1. To retrieve all tuples of employees whose age is greater than 30 from an "Employee" relation, the query can be written as:

   { T | T ∈ Employee ∧ T.age > 30 }

2. To retrieve the names of all employees working in the "HR" department.

   { T.Name | T ∈ Employee ∧ T.Department = "HR" }

3. Retrieve the IDs of employees who earn more than 50,000.

   { T.Emp_ID | T ∈ Employee ∧ T.Salary > 50000 }

4. Retrieve the names and ages of employees who are older than 40.

   { <T.Name, T.Age> | T ∈ Employee ∧ T.Age > 40 }

5. Retrieve the names of employees who do not work in the "Sales" department.

   { T.Name | T ∈ Employee ∧ T.Department ≠ "Sales" }

6. Retrieve employee IDs of employees who work in the same department as "John".

   { T1.Emp_ID | T1 ∈ Employee ∧ ∃ T2

   (T2 ∈ Employee ∧ T2.Name = "John"

   ∧ T1.Department = T2.Department) }

Domain Relational Calculus

In Domain Relational Calculus, instead of using tuples, it works with domain variables, which take on values from an attribute's domain.

The result is defined by conditions on these attribute values.

The syntax of a TRC expression is:

{ <x1, x2, ..., xn> | P(x1, x2, ..., xn) }

Explanation of Syntax Elements

- Domain Variables (x1, x2, ..., xn)

  Domain variables represent the values of individual attributes (fields) in a relation.

  These variables are used to represent the values in specific columns of a table.

  For example,

  > if you have a relation Employee(Emp_ID, Name, Age, Department, Salary), each column value can be represented by a domain variable like e_id, e_name, e_age, e_dept, e_salary.

- Predicates (P)

  A predicate specifies a logical condition that must be satisfied by the domain variables.

  The predicate can involve logical connectives like AND ($\land$), OR ($\lor$), NOT ($\neg$), comparisons ($=$, $\neq$, $<$, $>$, etc.), and quantifiers like Existential Quantifier ($\exists$) and Universal Quantifier ($\forall$).

  Example of a Predicate:

  > For a query like "Find the names of employees who work in the HR department":

  > P(e_id, e_name, e_age, e_dept, e_salary) = e_dept = "HR"

- Existential Quantifier ($\exists$)

  $\exists$ means "there exists". It asserts that a specific value or set of values exists that satisfies the condition.

  Example

  $\exists$ e_salary (e_salary > 50000)

  This means that there exists a salary greater than 50,000.

- Universal Quantifier ($\forall$)

  $\forall$ means "for all". It ensures that the condition holds true for all values of the variable.

  Example

  $\forall$ e_salary (e_salary < 100000)

  This means all employee salaries are less than 100,000.

Formula Structure

The formula (P) can be constructed using several elements:

- Comparison Operators: To compare values. These include:

  $=, \neq, <, >, \leq, \geq$

- Logical Operators: These include:

  - AND ($\land$): Combines multiple conditions that must all be true.

  - OR ($\lor$): Specifies that at least one of the conditions must be true.

  - NOT ($\neg$): Negates a condition.

- Quantifiers: Existential ($\exists$) and universal ($\forall$) quantifiers specify whether something exists or applies to all values.

We will use a sample relation called Employee with the following schema to understand Domain Relational Calculus with examples.

Employee(Emp_ID, Name, Age, Department, Salary)

1. Retrieve the names of employees working in the "HR" department.

   { <e_name> | ∃ e_id, e_age, e_salary

   (<e_id, e_name, e_age, "HR", e_salary> ∈ Employee) }

   Explanation:

   - o e_name: This is the domain variable representing the employee's name, which will be part of the result set.

   - o ∃ e_id, e_age, e_salary: These are the existential quantifiers for the other attributes. We're not retrieving them but specifying that they exist.

   - o <e_id, e_name, e_age, "HR", e_salary>: This specifies a tuple in the Employee relation where the department is "HR".

2. Retrieve the IDs of employees who earn more than 50,000.

   { <e_id> | ∃ e_name, e_age, e_dept, e_salary

   (<e_id, e_name, e_age, e_dept, e_salary >

   ∈ Employee ∧ e_salary > 50000) }

   Explanation:

   - o e_id: The domain variable representing the employee ID, which is the result of this query.

- o ∃ e_name, e_age, e_dept, e_salary: These variables are existentially quantified since we don't need them in the output but they exist.

- o <e_id, e_name, e_age, e_dept, e_salary>: Represents a tuple in the Employee relation.

- o e_salary > 50000: The condition to ensure only employees with a salary greater than 50,000 are selected.

4. Normalization

Functional Dependency

Functional Dependency essentially means that in a relation say R, the value of one attribute say A determines the value of another attribute (or set of attributes) say B,C.

Determines means

If A → C (read it as 'A determinant of C' or 'C functionally depend on A') then following condition must be present in relation R

Relation : R			
A	B	C	D
a1	b1	c1	d1
a1	b1	c1	d2
a2	b2	c3	d1
a2	b1	c3	d1

Table 4.1 Fucntional Dependancy

T1 (A) = (a1) &

T2 (A) = (a1)

Now consider

T1 (C) = C1

T2 (C) = C1

For example, consider a Relation Interview as shown IN Table 4.2

If (SUBJECT, INTERVIEWER) → ROOMNO then following condition must be present in relation INTERVIEW

T1 (SUBJECT, INTERVIEWER) = (Database, Sam)

&

T4 (SUBJECT, INTERVIEWER) = (Database, Sam)

Now consider

T1 (ROOMNO) = 205

T4 (ROOMNO) = 205

Therefore, we can say that

(SUBJECT, INTERVIEWER) → ROOMNO

Subject	Interviewer	RoomNo	Candidate
Database	Sam	205	Raj
Networking	John	208	Aman
Database	Sameer	207	Smith
Database	Sam	205	Rakesh

Table 4.2   INTERVIEW

Functional dependencies are important in database design and normalization because they help ensure data integrity and minimize redundancy.

Transitive Dependency

A transitive dependency occurs when a non-key attribute depends on another non-key attribute rather than directly on the primary key.

For example

For a relation R (A,B,C,D), if A is the primary key, and we have following dependencies

A → B

B → C

Here, C is transitively dependent on A through B, meaning C does not directly depend on the primary key A

Multivalued Dependency

A table exhibits multivalued dependency if:

- o A **Multivalued Dependency (MVD)** is a type of dependency in a relational database that occurs when one attribute in a table determines multiple independent sets of values of another attribute.

- o In simpler terms, if two attributes in a table are independent of each other but are both dependent on a third attribute, there is a multivalued dependency.

- o For a relation R(A,B,C) an MVD A→→B implies that for each value of A, there is a set of values for B, and this set is independent of the values in C.

let's consider a scenario with a relation, "Employees":

Employees (Emp_ID, Emp_Name, Emp_Skill, Emp_Language)

In above table schema

Emp_ID determines the Emp_Skill of the employee.

Emp_ID also determines the Emp_Language the employee speaks.

But the Emp_Skill and Emp_Language attributes are independent of each other. The skills a person has are unrelated to the languages they speak.

Multivalued Dependency in This Example:

EmpID $\rightarrow\rightarrow$ Emp_Skill: For each EmpID, there are multiple skills.

EmpID $\rightarrow\rightarrow$ Emp_Language: For each EmpID, there are multiple languages.

However, the skills and languages are independent of each other.

Normalization

Normalization is a process used in database design to organize data efficiently and reduce redundancy. It involves breaking down large tables into smaller, related tables and defining relationships between them. The main objectives of normalization are to eliminate data redundancy, ensure data integrity, and make the database structure more flexible and adaptable to changes.

Normalization Forms

Normalization typically involves several normal forms, each addressing specific issues related to data redundancy and dependency. The most commonly used normal forms are:

1. First Normal Form (1NF)

2. Second Normal Form (2NF)

3. Third Normal Form (3NF)

4. Boyce-Codd Normal Form (BCNF)

5. Fourth Normal Form (4NF)

First Normal Form (1NF)

Ensures that each column in a table contains atomic values and that there are no repeating groups of columns.

Consider course_enrolled relation as follows, course_enrolled relation is not in 1NF, Because courseID, courseName and InstructorName attribute is not an atomic attribute and consist multiple values.

studentID	courseID	studentName	courseName	InstructorName
1	C101, C102	Aman	Math, Physics	Prof. John, Prof. Smith
2	C101, C103	Sameer	Math, Chemistry	Prof. John, Prof Adam

Table 4.3 course_enrolled (Not in 1NF)

To bring a table into 1NF, you may need to:

- o Break down columns containing multiple values into separate columns.

- o Remove any repeating groups by creating new tables and establishing relationships between them using primary and foreign keys.

- o Ensure that each column has a unique name and contains atomic values.

Here is a solution for our example:

studentID	courseID	studentName	courseName	InstructorName
1	C101	Aman	Maths	Prof. John
1	C102	Aman	Physics	Prof. Smith
2	C101	Sameer	Maths	Prof. John
2	C103	Sameer	Chemistry	Prof. Adam

Table 4.4 course_enrolled (in 1NF)

Now relation course_enrolled is in 1NF

Second Normal Form (2NF)

A database table is said to be in 2NF if it satisfies the following conditions:

- o It is in First Normal Form (1NF): All the attributes must have atomic (indivisible) values, and the table must not have any repeating groups.

o There is no partial dependency: This means that all non-key (non-prime) attributes must depend on the whole primary key, not just a part of it. In other words, in tables where the primary key is a composite key (a primary key made up of more than one column), non-key attributes must depend on all parts of the composite key, not just a subset of it.

Consider a table that stores information about students and the courses they are enrolled in:

studentID	courseID	studentName	courseName	InstructorName
1	C101	Aman	Maths	Prof. John
1	C102	Aman	Physics	Prof. Smith
2	C101	Sameer	Maths	Prof. John
2	C103	Sameer	Chemistry	Prof. Adam

Table 4.5 course_enrolled (in 1NF)

Primary key: (StudentID, CourseID) – since a student can take multiple courses.

The **non-key (non-prime)** attributes are StudentName, CourseName, and InstructorName.

In this table:

o StudentName depends only on StudentID.

o CourseName and InstructorName depend only on CourseID.

This means that there are partial dependencies, where non-key attributes depend on only a part of the composite key (StudentID, CourseID), which violates 2NF.

To remove partial dependencies, we decompose the table into three tables:

1. Student Table (contains details related to students with studentID as primary key).

2. Course Table (contains details related to courses with courseID as primary key).

3. Student_Course (to track which students are enrolled in which courses).

StudentID	studentName
1	Aman
2	Sameer

Table 4.5.1: student

CourseID	CourseName	InstructorName
C101	Math	Prof. John
C102	Physics	Prof. Smith
C103	Chemistry	Prof. Adam

Table 4.5.2: course

StudentID	courseID
1	C101
1	C102
2	C101
2	C103

Table 4.5.3: student_course

Third Normal Form (3NF)

A database table is said to be in 3NF if it satisfies the following conditions:

o   It is in Second Normal Form (2NF).

o   There is no transitive dependency: This means that non-key attributes must depend directly on the primary key and not on another non-key attribute. In other words, there should be no indirect dependency of any column on the primary key.

Consider a table that stores department-head information.

deptID	deptName	deptHeadID	deptHeadName
D1	Computer	H1	Prof. Rafeh
D2	Mechanical	H2	Prof. Zain

Table 4.6: department-head

Here, a transitive dependency does exist because:

o   The deptID determines the deptHeadID, and

o   The deptHeadID determines the deptHeadName.

This means that deptID transitively determines deptHeadName through deptHeadID. In other words, the dependency from deptID to deptHeadName is indirect, going through deptHeadID.

How to Resolve the Transitive Dependency:

To remove the transitive dependency, we can split the table into two separate tables:

1. Department Table (Stores department-related information):

2. Head Table (Stores head-related information):

deptID	deptName	deptHeadID
D1	Computer	H1
D2	Mechanical	H2

Table 4.6.1: Department

deptHeadID	deptHeadName
H1	Prof. Rafeh
H2	Prof. Zain

Table 4.6.2: Head

This decomposition ensures that the tables are in Third Normal Form (3NF), eliminating transitive dependencies and making the database more efficient.

Boyce-Codd Normal Form (BCNF)

The BCNF is an advanced version of the Third Normal Form (3NF). BCNF is designed to address certain anomalies that 3NF may not resolve, particularly in tables with composite keys or situations where non-prime attributes (attributes not part of any candidate key) depend on part of a candidate key.

A relation (table) is in BCNF if it meets the following two conditions:

o   It is in 3NF, meaning it satisfies all the rules of 3NF.

o   Every non-trivial functional dependency has a superkey as its determinant. In other words, for any functional dependency $X \rightarrow Y$, X must be a superkey of the table. (A superkey is a set of one or more attributes that can uniquely identify a row in a table.)

Consider a university course assignment table:

course	Instructor	Time
Math	Prof. Aman	09AM
Physics	Prof. Sam	10AM
Math	Prof. Aman	11AM

Table 4.7: course_time

Functional Dependencies in the Table:

1. Course $\rightarrow$ Instructor: Each course is taught by only one instructor.

2. Course, Time $\rightarrow$ Instructor: The combination of course and time uniquely determines the instructor.

However, this table is not in BCNF because the functional dependency

Course $\rightarrow$ Instructor exists, but Course is not a superkey (since Course alone does not uniquely identify each row; we also need Time).

We need to decompose the table to eliminate the non-superkey dependency.

Course-Instructor Table

course	Instructor
Math	Prof. Aman
Physics	Prof. Sam

Table 4.7.1: course_instructor

Course-Time Table:

course	Time
Math	09AM
Physics	10AM

Math	11AM

Table 4.7.2: course_time

Fourth Normal Form (4NF)

Fourth Normal Form is more restrictive than BCNF. We shall see that every 4NF schema is also in BCNF, but there are BCNF schemas that are not in 4NF.

Redundancy caused by multi-valued dependencies can be addressed by 4NF.

4NF ensures that the database is free from non-trivial multi-valued dependencies.

A table is in 4NF if it meets the following conditions:

- It is in Boyce-Codd Normal Form (BCNF), which ensures that all functional dependencies are preserved.

- There are no non-trivial multi-valued dependencies: A multi-valued dependency occurs when one attribute in a table determines multiple independent values of another attribute.

Table Before 4NF (With Multi-Valued Dependencies):

Emp_ID	Emp_Skill	Emp_Language
101	React	English
101	Django	English
101	React	Arabic
101	Django	Arabic
102	Angular	French
102	Bootstrap	French

Table 4.8: Employee

Here, we can see that for Emp_ID = 101, there are multiple skills (React, Django) and multiple languages (English, Arabic). The skills and languages are independent of each other, but they are both dependent on Emp_ID. This results in redundant data, as we store every combination of skills and languages for the same employee multiple times.

54

Due to following Multivalued dependencies a given relation is not in 4NF.

EmpID →→ Skill

EmpID →→ Language

Conversion to 4NF (Removing Multi-Valued Dependencies)

To remove the multi-valued dependencies and bring the table into 4NF, we can split the table into two separate tables:

Employee Skills Table

Emp_ID	Emp_Skill
101	React
101	Django
102	Angular
102	Bootstrap

Table 4.8.1: Employee_skill

Employee Languages Table

Emp_ID	Emp_Language
101	English
101	Arabic
102	French

Table 4.8.2: Employee_language

5. SQL – A Practical Approach

SQL Introduction

SQL (Structured Query Language) is the standard programming language used to manage and manipulate relational databases. It allows users to perform a wide range of operations, including querying data, updating records, creating and modifying database structures, and managing access to data.

IBM created the first version of SQL, which was originally called Sequel, in the early 1970s as part of the System R project. Over time, Sequel evolved, and its name changed to SQL (Structured Query Language). Today, many products support SQL, and it has become the standard language for relational databases.

Characteristics of SQL

Declarative Language

SQL is a declarative language, meaning that users specify what they want from the database (e.g., retrieve data, insert data) rather than how the operations should be performed.

Non-procedural

Users describe the result they want, and the DBMS figures out the best way to get it.

Standardized

ANSI (American National Standards Institute) and ISO (International Organization for Standardization) have standardized SQL, although many database systems implement their own extensions (e.g., MySQL, Oracle, and Microsoft SQL Server).

Data Independence

SQL allows data abstraction and data independence. This means changes in the database structure (like adding columns) do not require changes in existing SQL queries, maintaining compatibility with different layers of the database.

Data Manipulation and Retrieval

SQL provides powerful commands for:

Data Retrieval

Using SELECT queries to retrieve specific data.

Data Manipulation

Using INSERT, UPDATE, and DELETE to modify data.

Data Filtering

Using WHERE clauses to filter specific records.

Multi-Table Queries (Joins)

SQL supports queries across multiple tables using joins (INNER JOIN, LEFT JOIN, RIGHT JOIN, FULL JOIN), allowing complex data retrieval from relational databases.

Set-Based Operations

SQL treats data as sets and allows operations on sets of data. SQL operations like UNION, INTERSECT, and EXCEPT allow for combining and comparing datasets.

Flexibility in Data Management

SQL allows you to define, create, modify, and delete database structures and data, offering complete flexibility for database management. This includes creating tables, defining constraints, and enforcing rules.

Support for Transactions

SQL supports transaction control to ensure data integrity. Commands like COMMIT, ROLLBACK, and SAVEPOINT help manage transactions and ensure that the database remains in a consistent state.

Security Features

SQL includes security features to control access to data using Data Control Language (DCL). You can define access rights using GRANT and REVOKE commands to restrict or allow users to perform certain operations.

Advantages of SQL

Extensibility

Most modern SQL systems support extensions beyond the standard SQL language, including procedural elements (like stored procedures, triggers, and functions) to add more logic and automation within the database.

Scalability

Supports Large Databases: SQL can manage and scale with massive amounts of data, making it suitable for small applications as well as large enterprise systems.

SQL Data Type

SQL provides various data types to define the kind of data that can be stored in a table's columns. These data types ensure that the correct type of data is entered and help in organizing, processing, and retrieving data efficiently. SQL data types can be broadly categorized as follows

Numeric Data Types

Horizontal and Vertical Scaling: SQL-based databases can be scaled both vertically (more powerful servers) and horizontally (distributed databases).

INT (Integer)

Memory Size: 4 bytes (32 bits)

Range:

Signed: -2,147,483,648 to 2,147,483,647

Unsigned: 0 to 4,294,967,295

SMALLINT

Memory Size: 2 bytes (16 bits)

Range:

Signed: -32,768 to 32,767

Unsigned: 0 to 65,535

BIGINT

Memory Size: 8 bytes (64 bits)

Range:

Signed: -9,223,372,036,854,775,808 to 9,223,372,036,854,775,807

Unsigned: 0 to 18,446,744,073,709,551,615

TINYINT

Memory Size: 1 byte (8 bits)

Range:

Signed: -128 to 127

Unsigned: 0 to 255

FLOAT

Memory Size: 4 or 8 bytes (platform-dependent).

FLOAT is used to store approximate floating-point numbers. Depending on the system, it can use 4 bytes (single precision) or 8 bytes (double precision).

Approximate numeric values, with a wide range for both large and small numbers.

REAL

Memory Size: 4 bytes (32 bits).

REAL is a single-precision floating-point number, typically using 4 bytes. It offers less precision compared to DOUBLE.

Range: Stores approximate values with less precision than DOUBLE.

DOUBLE

Memory Size: 8 bytes (64 bits).

DOUBLE is a double-precision floating-point number, offering greater precision and range than REAL.

Range: Suitable for storing large or very precise floating-point numbers.

NUMERIC(P,S)

Memory Size: Depends on the precision p (total number of

digits) and scale s (number of digits after the decimal point). Each digit requires about 1 byte of storage.

NUMERIC is used for exact precision numbers, often for financial or monetary values. It stores values precisely, avoiding rounding errors.

Example:

NUMERIC(10, 2) will allocate approximately 10 bytes to store the value.

DECIMAL(P, S)

Memory Size: Similar to NUMERIC, memory usage depends on the precision p and scale s.

Each digit requires about 1 byte of storage.

DECIMAL is similar to NUMERIC, used for exact numeric values. It is typically interchangeable with NUMERIC.

Example:

DECIMAL(10, 2) will allocate approximately 10 bytes (10 digits total size including 2 digits after decimal point)

Character Data Types

CHAR(N)

Allocates n bytes, where n is the number of characters.

CHAR is a fixed-length data type. If you store fewer characters than n, the rest of the space is padded with spaces.

Example:

CHAR(10) always takes 10 bytes, even if only 5 characters are stored.

VARCHAR(N)

Allocates the actual number of characters stored, plus 1 or 2 bytes for length information.

1 byte for lengths up to 255 characters.

2 bytes for lengths over 255 characters.

VARCHAR is a variable-length data type. Only the number of characters stored, plus the overhead for length information, is allocated.

SQL commands

SQL (Structured Query Language) commands are categorized into various types based on their purpose. Here's an overview of the main types and their respective commands:

- o   DDL (Data Definition Language)
- o   DML(Data Manipulation Language)
- o   DCL (Data Control Language)
- o   DQL (Data Query Language)

Data Definition Language (DDL)

DDL (Data Definition Language) commands are used in SQL (Structured Query Language) to define or modify the structure of a database, including creating, altering, and deleting database objects like tables, indexes, and views.

List of DDL Commands;

1. Create

2. Alter - (add, modify, drop)

3. Rename

4. Drop

5. Truncate

6. Desc

CREATE COMMAND

The CREATE command is used to create new database objects such as tables, views, indexes, or schemas.

```
Syntax

CREATE TABLE table_name
( column_name1 data_type(size) constraints,
column_name2 data_type(size) constraints,
...
);
```

```
Example

CREATE TABLE Employees
(
EmployeeID INT PRIMARY KEY,
FirstName VARCHAR(50) NOT NULL,
LastName VARCHAR(50),
BirthDate DATE,
HireDate DATE,
Salary DECIMAL(10, 2)
);
```

In above example we have created an Employees table with multiple columns of different type and size.

After create command we can display the schema of a relation/table by using describe or desc command as follows

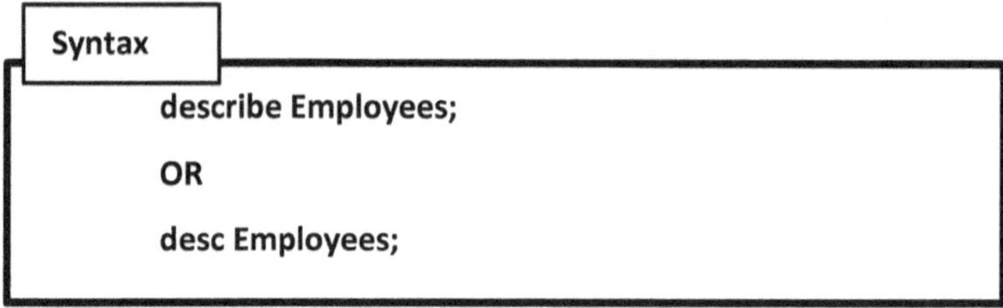

ALTER COMMAND

It used to change the schema of the database. There are three clauses in which we may apply in alter command.

- o add clause : to add new column (with constraint if any).

- o modify clause : to modify existing column.

- o drop clause : to remove a column from a table.

- o rename clause : to change name of existing a column.

Alter Command Using ADD Clause

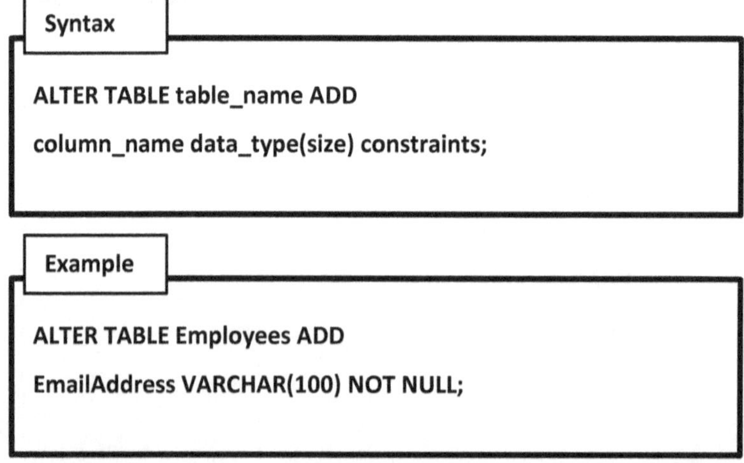

In above example we have added a new column EmailAddress with size 100 characters, and a NOT NULL constraint to make a column value compulsory.

You can check new column added or not by running desc command as discussed above.

Alter Command Using MODIFY Clause

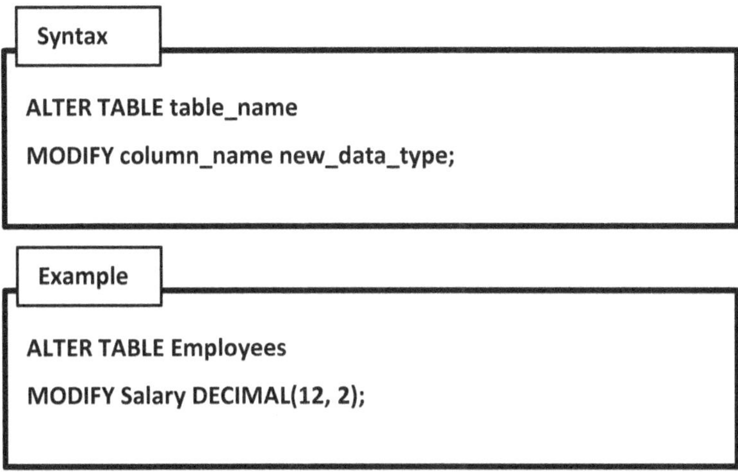

In above example we modified an existing column Salary with a new size.

(Refer Decimal datatype explanation for better understanding).

You can check column with new size by running desc command as discussed above.

Alter Command Using Drop Clause

```
Example

ALTER TABLE Employees DROP COLUMN EmailAddress;
```

Above command after successful execution will remove EmailAddress column from a table

Run a desc command to check whether column removed or not.

Alter Command Using rename Clause

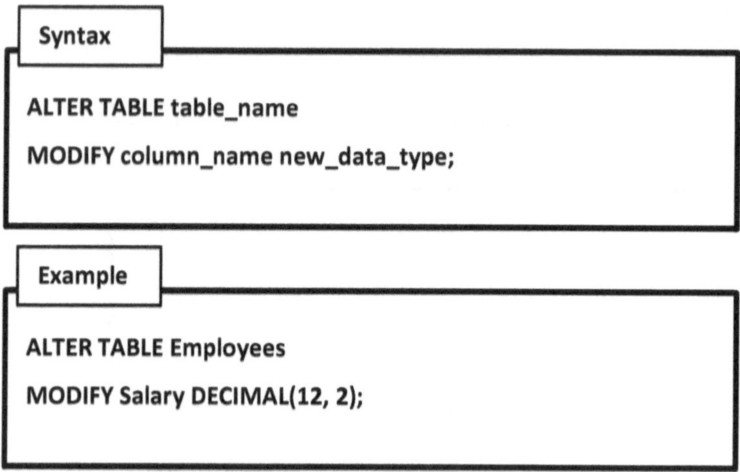

```
Syntax

ALTER TABLE table_name

MODIFY column_name new_data_type;
```

```
Example

ALTER TABLE Employees

MODIFY Salary DECIMAL(12, 2);
```

Above command after successful execution will rename HireDate (old column name) to JoinDate (new column name).

Run a desc command to check whether column name changed or not.

RENAME COMMAND

The RENAME command is used to rename a database object such as a table.

```
Syntax

RENAME old_table_name TO new_table_name;
```

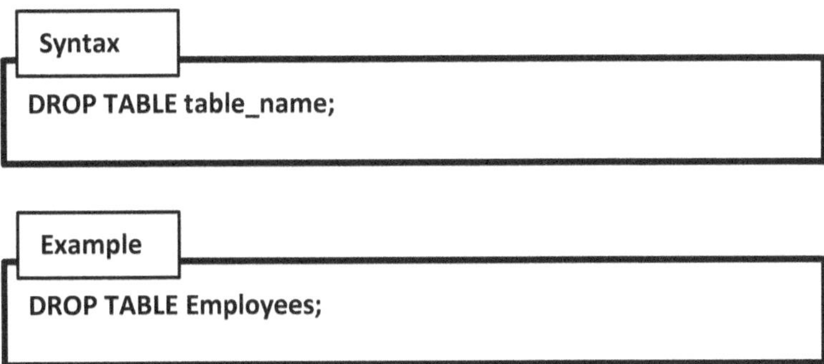

It will change old table name (Employees) with a new table name (Staff). Now we are not able use old name. to describe table now use new name Staff.

DROP COMMAND

This command deletes the Employees table structure from database, including all its data.

TRUNCATE COMMAND

The TRUNCATE command is used to remove all rows from a table, but it keeps the table structure intact. It is faster than the DELETE command because it does not log individual row deletions.

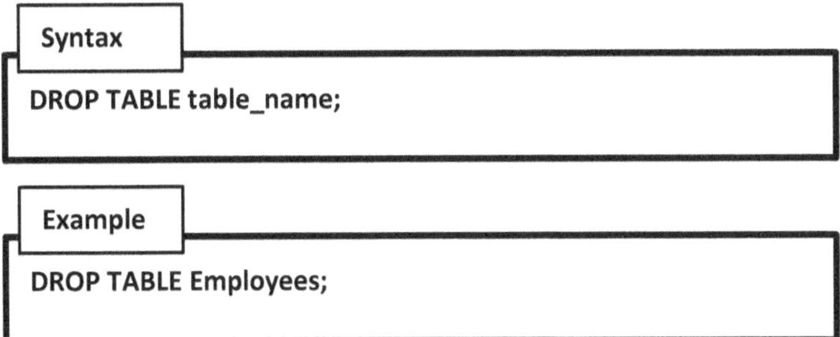

This removes all records from the Employees table, but the table still exists.

DESC COMMAND

Desc or Describe command is used to display structure of database table object.

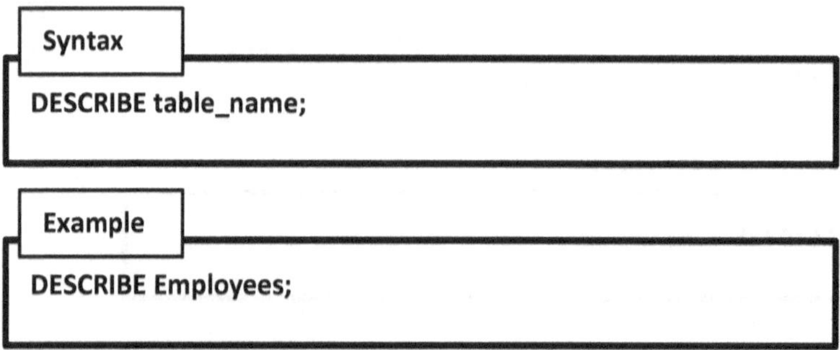

This command will display schema or structure of Employees table.

Data Manipulation Language (DML)

Data Manipulation Language (DML) commands are a subset of SQL (Structured Query Language) used to manipulate data in relational databases. DML commands allow users to retrieve, insert, update, and delete data from database tables.

The most common DML commands are:

- o INSERT: Adds new rows of data into a table.

- o UPDATE: Modifies existing data in a table.

- o DELETE: Removes existing data from a table.

INSERT COMMAND

The INSERT statement is used to add new records to a table.

┌─ **Syntax** ───────────────────────────────────┐

```
INSERT INTO table_name
(column1, column2, ...)
VALUES
(value1, value2, ...);
```

└──┘

table_name: The name of the table where the data will be inserted.

column1, column2: The specific columns where values are inserted.

value1, value2: The values to be inserted into the specified columns.

Example 1

INSERT INTO Employees

(E_id,Name, Age, City, JoinDate, Salary, Department)

VALUES

(6001,'John Smith', 35, 'New York', '2017-05-10', 75000, 'Sales');

This statement inserts a new row into the employees table with the values 'John Doe', 29, and 'New York' for the name, age, and city columns, respectively.

Column names in Insert command are optional if not mentioned, we have to maintain order of values as per column sequence in schema to avoid any logical error. For example

Example 2

INSERT INTO VALUES

(6002,'Sarah Johnson', 28, 'Los Angeles', '2019-08-21', 68000, 'Marketing');

Now insert all remaining data (refer following table) in employees relation.

e_id	Name	Age	City	Join Date	Salary	Department
6001	John Smith	35	New York	10-05-2017	75000	Sales
6002	Sarah Johnson	28	Los Angeles	21-08-2019	68000	Marketing
6003	Michael Brown	42	Chicago	15-03-2015	95000	IT
6004	Emily Davis	31	Houston	04-11-2020	80000	Human Resources
6005	David Wilson	50	Phoenix	30-06-2013	120000	Finance
6006	Laura Martinez	26	San Francisco	12-09-2021	65000	Marketing
6007	James Anderson	38	Dallas	18-04-2016	85000	IT
6008	Olivia Garcia	29	Miami	10-01-2022	70000	Sales
6009	Robert Lee	45	Seattle	22-07-2014	110000	Finance
6010	Sophia White	33	Boston	28-02-2018	78000	Human Resources

Table 5.1: employees

UPDATE COMMAND

The UPDATE statement is used to modify existing records in a table.

Upadte command can be run without where clause (without condition) or with where clause (with condition).

Syntax

```
UPDATE table_name SET

column1 = value1, column2 = value2, ...

WHERE condition;
```

Example 1

```
UPDATE employees SET  age = 30, city = 'Chicago'

WHERE name = 'John Smith';
```

This statement updates the age and city values for the employee named 'John Doe', setting the age to 30 and the city to 'Chicago'.

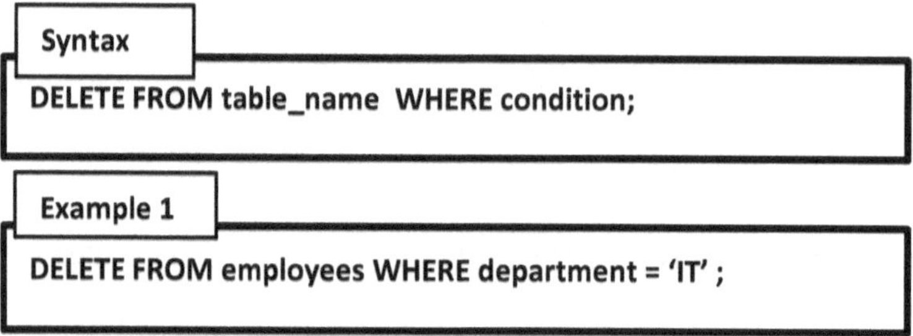

This statement updates the age and city values to 30, 'Chicago' respectively for all records of the employee table.

(*Don't run as your all records will affect, just try to understand the difference in Example1 and Example2*)

DELETE COMMAND

The DELETE statement removes records (rows) from a table.

This deletes all records from the employees table where the department is 'IT'.

(*Run it and see the change in table data by running select command, then after that insert again deleted records*)

This statement removes all records from employees table.

(*Don't run as it will delete all records from employees table which you will need to use in further examples*)

Data Query Language (DQL)

Data Query Language (DQL) commands are used to retrieve data from a database. In SQL, the primary command under DQL is the SELECT statement. It allows users to query one or more tables and retrieve specific data based on conditions.

SELECT COMMAND

The SELECT statement is used to query and retrieve data from one or more tables.

<table>
<tr><td>Syntax</td></tr>
<tr><td>

SELECT column1, column2, ...

FROM table_name

WHERE condition;

</td></tr>
</table>

column1, column2: The specific columns you want to retrieve.

table_name: The name of the table from which to fetch the data.

condition: Optional, Used to filter the results (e.g., WHERE age > 30).

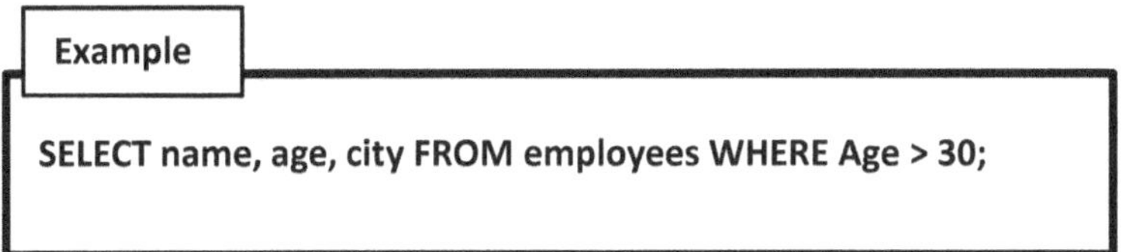

<table>
<tr><td>Example</td></tr>
<tr><td>

SELECT name, age, city FROM employees WHERE Age > 30;

</td></tr>
</table>

This query retrieves the name, age, and city columns of all employees older than 30 from the employees table.

Data Control Language (DCL)

Data Control Language (DCL) commands in SQL are used to control access to the database. These commands manage permissions and access rights for users to ensure database security.

In SQL, privileges refer to the rights granted to users to perform specific actions on database objects or perform administrative tasks. Privileges are broadly categorized into system privileges and object privileges.

Privileges in DCL

System Privileges

System privileges allow users to perform administrative actions or affect the database schema. These privileges apply globally across the database and are typically granted to database administrators or users who need elevated permissions.

CREATE SESSION	Allows the user to log in to the database.
CREATE TABLE	Allows the user to create new tables.
DROP TABLE	Allows the user to drop tables.
CREATE VIEW	Allows the user to create views.
CREATE USER	Allows the user to create new database users.
DROP USER	Allows the user to delete database users.
ALTER USER	Allows the user to modify user attributes.
DROP ANY TABLE	Allows the user to drop tables in any schema.

Object Privileges

Object privileges allow users to perform actions on specific database objects, such as tables, views, or procedures. These privileges are object-specific and do not apply globally.

SELECT	Allows the user to retrieve data from a table or view.
INSERT	Allows the user to insert data into a table.
UPDATE	Allows the user to update existing data in a table.
DELETE	Allows the user to delete data from a table.
EXECUTE	Allows the user to execute a stored procedure or function.
REFERENCES	Allows the user to create foreign keys that reference the specified table.
ALTER	Allows the user to alter a table or object.
INDEX	Allows the user to create indexes on a table.

GRANT

The GRANT command is used to give specific privileges or permissions to a user or a group of users.

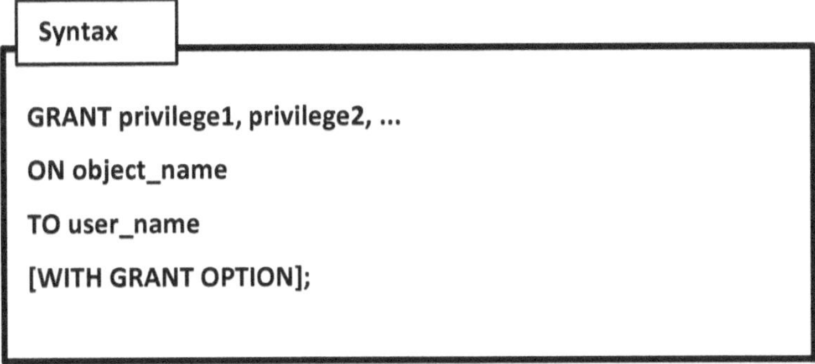

Key Points:

- o **privileges:** Actions like SELECT, INSERT, UPDATE, DELETE, etc.

- o **object_name:** The database object (e.g., table, view).

- o **WITH GRANT OPTION:** Allows the user to grant the same permissions to other users.

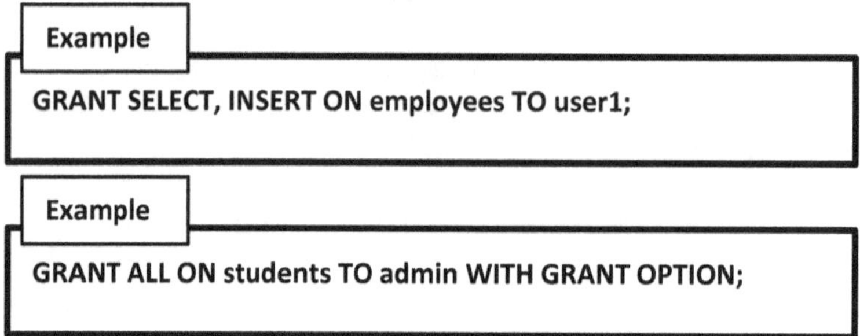

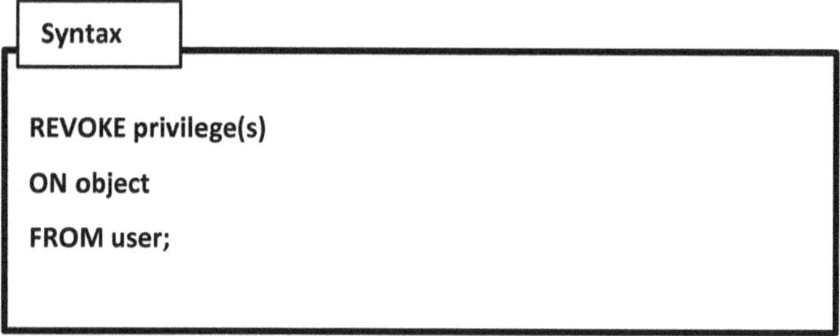

REVOKE

The REVOKE command is used to remove previously granted permissions from a user or role.

Key Points:

- o Removes specific permissions.

- o Can only revoke permissions previously granted.

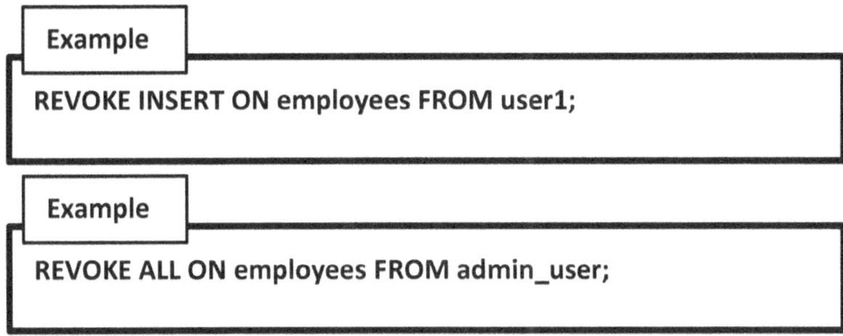

Integrity Constraints using SQL

Primary Key Constraint

It is used to uniquely define a record. None of the fields that are part of the primary key can contain a null value. A table can have only one primary key.

There Are Two Ways Of Applying primary key

- o At the time of table creation

- o After table creation

At the time of table creation


```
CREATE TABLE Students
(       StudentID INT PRIMARY KEY,
        RollNo NUMBER (3),
        Name VARCHAR(50),
        Age INT
);
```

┌─────────┐
│ Example │
└─────────┴──────────────────────────────────┐
│   │
│ **ALTER TABLE Students**   │
│   │
│ **ADD**   │
│   │
│ **PRIMARY KEY (RollNo);**   │
│   │
└───┘

This makes RollNo the primary key after table creation by using ALTER command, ensuring each value is unique and NOT NULL.

NOTE: this command will output an error message because more than one primary keys are not possible in one relation.

Unique Key

Ensures that all values in a column are unique.

Unlike the primary key, a table can have multiple columns with the UNIQUE constraint.

There are two ways of applying unique key.

- o   At the time of table creation
- o   After table creation

At the time of table creation

┌─────────┐
│ Example │
└─────────┴──────────────────────────────────┐
│   │
│ **CREATE TABLE Employees1**   │
│   │
│ **(**   │
│   │
│   **EmployeeID INT PRIMARY KEY,**   │
│   │
│   **Email VARCHAR(100) UNIQUE,**   │
│   │
│   **Name VARCHAR(50)**   │
│   │
│ **);**   │
│   │
└───┘

After the time of table creation

```
ALTER TABLE Employees1

ADD

UNIQUE (Email);
```

This ensures that the Email column has unique values when the table is created. (Two UNIQIUE KEYS are possible in one relation).

NOT NULL Constraint

Ensures that a column cannot have a NULL value.

There are two ways of applying NOT NULL key.

- o   At the time of table creation

- o   After table creation

At the time of table creation

```
CREATE TABLE Orders

(        OrderID INT PRIMARY KEY,

         ProductName VARCHAR(100) NOT NULL,

         Quantity INT  );
```

After the time of table creation

```
ALTER    TABLE Orders MODIFY

Quantity VARCHAR(100) NOT NULL;
```

This modifies the Quantity column to ensure it cannot contain NULL values after the table creation.

CHECK Constraint

Ensures that the values in a column meet a specific condition.

There are two ways of applying CHECK key.

- o   At the time of table creation

- o   After table creation

At the time of table creation

```
Example

CREATE TABLE Employees2
(         EmployeeID INT PRIMARY KEY,
          Age INT,
          Salary DECIMAL(10, 2) CHECK (Salary > 0)  );
```

After the time of table creation

```
Example

ALTER TABLE Employees2 ADD
CHECK (Age >= 18);
```

This adds a CHECK constraint on the Age column to ensure that values are 18 or older.

```
Example

CREATE TABLE Students
(         StudentID INT PRIMARY KEY, RollNo NUMBER (3),
          Name VARCHAR(50),  Age INT  );
```

FOREIGHN KEY Constraint

Establishes a relationship between two tables and ensures that the value in one table corresponds to a value in another table.

- o At the time of table creation
- o After table creation

At the time of table creation

```
Example

CREATE TABLE Orders
(        OrderID INT PRIMARY KEY,
         CustomerID INT,
         FOREIGN KEY (CustomerID)
         REFERENCES Customers(CustomerID)
);
```

After the time of table creation

```
Example

ALTER TABLE Orders
        ADD CONSTRAINT fk_customer
        FOREIGN KEY (CustomerID)
        REFERENCES Customers(CustomerID);
```

Here, CustomerID in the Orders table is a foreign key that references the CustomerID in the Customers table, ensuring that each order corresponds to an existing customer.

SQL Operators

SQL operators are used to perform operations on data, such as comparing values, performing arithmetic calculations, or manipulating data.

Below are the main types of SQL operators, along with descriptions and examples of their use:

Arithmetic Operators

These operators perform basic mathematical operations.

- o   Addition (+) ------------- Adds two values.

- o   Subtraction (-) ---------- Subtracts one value from another.

- o   Multiplication (*) ------ Multiplies two values.

- o   Division (/) --------------- Divides one value by another.

- o   Modulus (%) ----------- Returns the remainder when one value is divided by another.

```
Example

SELECT 10 + 5 AS AdditionResult FROM dual;    -- Result: 15

SELECT 10 - 5 AS SubtractionResult FROM dual; -- Result: 5

SELECT 10 * 5 AS MultiplicationResult FROM dual; -- Result: 50

SELECT 10 / 2 AS DivisionResult FROM dual;    -- Result: 5

SELECT 10 % 3 AS ModulusResult FROM dual;    -- Result: 1
```

To run above sql commands we used dual table.

The DUAL table in SQL is a special one-row, one-column table that exists in some database systems like Oracle. It is primarily used to perform operations or calculations that do not require an actual table or to retrieve system-level data.

Comparison Operators

These operators are used to compare two values and return a boolean result (TRUE or FALSE).

- Equal to (=): Checks if two values are equal.

- Not equal to (< > or !=): Checks if two values are not equal.

- Greater than (>): Checks if the first value is greater than the second.

- Less than (<): Checks if the first value is less than the second.

- Greater than or equal to (>=): Checks if the first value is greater than or equal to the second.

- Less than or equal to (<=): Checks if the first value is less than or equal to the second.

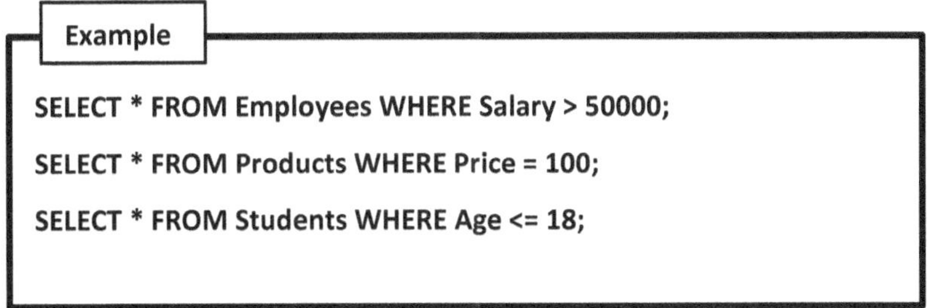

Logical Operators

Logical operators are used to combine multiple conditions in WHERE clauses.

- AND: Returns TRUE if all conditions are TRUE.

- OR: Returns TRUE if at least one condition is TRUE.

- NOT: Reverses the result of a condition.

Example

SELECT * FROM Employees WHERE

        Salary > 50000 AND Department = 'Sales';

SELECT * FROM Students WHERE Age < 18 OR Grade = 'A';

SELECT * FROM Orders WHERE NOT Status = 'Shipped';

BETWEEN Operator

Used to filter the result set within a specific range, also known as **range searching operator**.

It is inclusive, meaning it includes the start and end values.

Example

SELECT * FROM Products WHERE Price

        BETWEEN 100 AND 200;

SELECT * FROM Products WHERE Price

        NOT BETWEEN 100 AND 200;

First query will list out all products record whose price is in between 100 to 200.

Second query will list out all products record whose price is not in between 100 to 200.

IN Operator

Used to filter the result set based on a list of values, also known as List operators.

Checks if a value matches any value in a list.

> **Example**
>
> **SELECT * FROM Employees WHERE Department**
>
> **IN ('HR', 'Finance', 'Sales');**
>
> **SELECT * FROM Employees WHERE Department**
>
> **NOT IN ('HR', 'Finance', 'Sales');**

First query will list out all employees' record whose department is either 'HR' or 'Finance' or 'Sales'.

Second query will list out all employees' record whose department is not either 'HR' or 'Finance' or 'Sales'.

LIKE Operator

Used to search for a specified pattern in a column, also known as pattern matching operators.

Often used with wildcard characters, wildcard characters are percent (%) and single underscore (_). These characters are used to prepare a pattern.

% (percent)

Represents zero or more characters with any value.

_ (single underscore)

Represents exactly single character with any value.

Example

SELECT * FROM Employees WHERE Name LIKE 'J%';

-- Finds all employees whose names starting with 'J'

SELECT * FROM Employees WHERE Name LIKE '_a%';

-- Finds all employees whose names have 'a' as the second letter

SELECT * FROM Employees WHERE Name LIKE '_____';

-- Finds all employees having exactly 5 characters (5 underscores in pattern) in their name

NOT LIKE Operator

We can also invert the working of the LIKE operator by using the NOT operator with it. This returns a result set that doesn't match the given string pattern.

Example

SELECT * FROM Customers WHERE Name NOT LIKE 'J%';

-- Finds all customers whose names not starting with 'J'

SELECT * FROM Customers WHERE Name NOT LIKE '_a%';

-- Finds all customers whose names doesn't have 'a' as the second letter

SELECT * FROM Customers WHERE Name NOT LIKE '_____';

-- Finds all customers doesn't having exactly 5 characters (5 underscores in pattern) in their name

IS NULL and IS NOT NULL Operators

Used to check if a value is NULL (no value) or not.

Example

SELECT * FROM Employees WHERE ManagerID IS NULL;

-- Finds all employees who does not have any manager.

SELECT * FROM Orders WHERE DeliveryDate IS NOT NULL;

-- Finds all orders who delivery date is present.

SQL Functions

SQL has two types of functions built in functions and user defined functions. User defined functions are defined by user by using PL/SQL programming. In this section, we are going to discuss SQL built-in Functions.

SQL Built in functions are ready to use, User just to know how to use it in SQL command.

SQL programming provides several built in functions to perform various operations on database. SQL built in functions are divided into different categories as follows.

- o   Arithmetic Functions

- o   String Functions

- o   Date and Time Functions

- o   Aggregate Functions

Arithmetic Functions

These functions perform basic mathematical operations.

- o abs(number) - Returns the absolute (positive) value of a number.

- o ceil(number) - Rounds a number up to the nearest integer.

- o floor(number) - Rounds a number down to the nearest integer.

- o exp(number) - Returns e raised to the power of the specified number, where e is Euler's number

- o power(base, raised_to) - Raises a number to the power of another number.

- o sqrt(number) - Returns the square root of a number.

  mod(num1,num2) -Returns the remainder of the division of two numbers.

```
Example

SELECT abs(-20) AS abs_Result FROM dual;    -- Result: 20

SELECT ceil(2.1) AS ceil_Result FROM dual; -- Result: 3

SELECT floor(3.9) AS floor_Result FROM dual; -- Result: 3

SELECT exp(3) AS expResult FROM dual;    -- Result: 20.08

SELECT power(4,2) AS powerResult FROM dual;    -- Result: 16

SELECT sqrt(64) AS sqrtResult FROM dual;    -- Result: 8

SELECT mod(17,3) AS modResult FROM dual;    -- Result: 2
```

String Functions

String functions in SQL are used to manipulate and process string (text) data. These functions help in modifying, formatting, extracting, and searching within string values stored in a database. Below are some commonly used SQL string functions with descriptions and examples.

LOWER( )	
Description	Returns a given input string into lowercase letters.
Syntax	LOWER(string)
Arguments	One argument of string type.
Return type	Returns a string type value.
Example	SELECT LOWER('rdBMS') from dual;
Output	rdbms

UPPER( )	
Description	Returns a given input string into uppercase letters.
Syntax	UPPER(string)
Arguments	One argument of string type.
Return type	Returns a string type value.
Example	SELECT UPPER('rdBMS') from dual;
Output	RDBMS

INITCAP( )	
Description	Converts the first letter of each word in a string to uppercase, and the rest to lowercase.
Syntax	INITCAP(string)
Arguments	One argument of string type.
Return type	Returns a string type value.
Example	SELECT INITCAP('hello world') from dual;
Output	Hello World

CONCAT( )	
Description	Combines two strings into one.
Syntax	CONCAT(string1,string2)
Arguments	Two arguments of string type.
Return type	Returns a string type value.
Example	SELECT CONCAT('Hello', ' World') from dual;
Output	HelloWorld

SUBSTR( )	
Description	Extracts a substring from a string starting at a specific position and for a specified length.
Syntax	SUBSTR(string, start_position, length)
Arguments	string argument is a main string from which we want to extract a substring.

	start_position indicates from which position you want to extract. length indicates how much characters you want to extract.
Return type	Returns a string type value.
Example	SELECT SUBSTR('POLYCLINIC', 5, 4) from dual;
Output	CLIN

INSTR( )	
Description	To find a substring in a main string, it returns the position of a substring within a string. If not found, returns 0.
Syntax	INSTR(string,substring)
Arguments	Two arguments of string type. string argument represents, string in which we want to find out. substring represents string that we want to find out. Strings values are case sensitive.
Return type	Returns a number type value that indicates position of a substring in a string.
Example	select INSTR('polyclinic','clinic') from dual; select INSTR('polyclinic','Clinic') from dual;
Output	5 -- clinic is at position 5 in polyclinic. 0 -- Clinic is not present in polyclinic.

LENGTH( )	
Description	Returns the length of a string.
Syntax	LENGTH(string)
Arguments	One argument of string type.
Return type	Returns a number type value.
Example	select LENGTH('rdBMS') from dual;
Output	5

LPAD( ) / RPAD( )	
Description	Pads the left side of a string with a specified character to a specified length.
Syntax	LPAD(string, length, pad_string)
Arguments	string in which we want to pad some specified character. length indicates maximum length. pad_string represents character that to be pad.
Return type	Returns a string type value.
Example	SELECT LPAD('DBMS', 7, '*') from dual; SELECT LPAD('DBMS', 4, '*') from dual; SELECT LPAD('DBMS', 3, '*') from dual;
Output	***DBMS DBMS DBM

LTRIM( ) / RTRIM( )	
Description	Removes leading characters (spaces by default) from a string.
Syntax	LTRIM(string, trim_string)
Arguments	Two string type arguments.
Return type	Returns a string type value by converting input string into lowercase.

Example	select LTRIM('polyclinic','po') from dual;
	select LTRIM('polyclinic','abc') from dual;
	select LTRIM(' polyclinic') from dual;

Output	lyclinic — 'po' is trimmed. polyclinic -- 'abc' not found. Polyclinic – by default spaces are trimmed.

TRIM( )	
Description	Removes leading and trailing spaces.
Syntax	TRIM(string)
Arguments	One argument of string type.
Return type	Returns a string type value.
Example	select TRIM(' POLY ') from dual;
Output	POLY

REPLACE( )	
Description	Replaces occurrences of a substring with another substring in a main string.
Syntax	REPLACE(original_string, substring_to_replace, replacement_string)
Arguments	original_string: The string in which you want to replace a substring. substring_to_replace: The substring you want to replace. replacement_string: The substring you want to use as a replacement.
Return type	Returns a string type value after replacement.
Example	SELECT REPLACE('NYD Office', 'NYD', 'New Delhi City') from dual; SELECT REPLACE('Hello World', 'World', ' ') from dual;

	SELECT REPLACE('abcabcabc', 'abc', 'xyz') from dual;
Output	New Delhi City Office Hello -- replaces with empty characters xyzxyzxyz -- multiple replacements

REVERSE( )	
Description	Returns a given input string into lowercase letters.
Syntax	LOWER(string)
Arguments	One argument of string type.
Return type	Returns a string type value by converting input string into lowercase.
Example	select lower('rdBMS') from dual;
Output	rdbms

Date/Time Functions

These functions perform basic date and Time operations.

SYSDATE	
Description	Returns the current system date.
Syntax	SYSDATE
Arguments	No Arguments
Return type	Returns a date type value.
Example	SELECT SYSDATE from dual;
Output	11-DEC-24

NEXT_DAY( )	
Description	Returns the date of the next occurrence of a specified day of the week after a given date.
Syntax	NEXT_DAY(date, day_of_week)
Arguments	date argument is a start date, day_of_week is a string representing the name of the weekday .
Return type	Returns a date type value.
Example	SELECT NEXT_DAY(SYSDATE, 'FRIDAY') from dual;
Output	13-DEC-24

ADD_MONTHS( )	
Description	Returns a new date after adding a specified number of months to a given date.

Syntax	ADD_MONTHS(date, number_of_months)
Arguments	date is a starting date, number_of_months is number of months to add (positive or negative).
Return type	Returns a date type value.
Example	SELECT ADD_MONTHS(SYSDATE, 2) from dual; SELECT ADD_MONTHS(SYSDATE, -2) from dual;
Output	11-FEB-25 11-OCT-24

LAST_DAY( )

Description	Returns the date of last day of the month for a given date.
Syntax	LAST_DAY(date)
Arguments	One argument of date type.
Return type	Returns a date type value.
Example	SELECT LAST_DAY(sysdate) from dual;
Output	31-DEC-24

MONTHS_BETWEEN( )

Description	Calculates the number of months (and fractional months) between two dates.
Syntax	MONTHS_BETWEEN(date1, date2)
Arguments	Two date type arguments. The date1 is later date and the date2 is earlier date respectively.
Return type	Returns a decimal value representing months.
Example	SELECT MONTHS_BETWEEN(to_date('12-01-2024','MM-DD-YYYY'), to_date('06-01-2024','MM-DD-YYYY')) AS months_difference from dual;
Output	MONTHS_DIFFERENCE ----------------- 6

LEAST( )

Description	Returns the smallest (earliest) date among a list of dates.
Syntax	LEAST(date1, date2, date3, ...)
Arguments	Multiple date type arguments.
Return type	Returns a date type value.
Example	SELECT LEAST(to_date('12-01-2024','MM-DD-YYYY'), to_date('06-01-2024','MM-DD-YYYY'), to_date('06-01-2023','MM-DD-YYYY')

	) AS earlier_date from dual;
Output	EARLIER_DATE --------- 01-JUN-23
GREATEST( )	
Description	Returns the greatest (later) date among a list of dates.
Syntax	GREATEST(date1, date2, date3, ...)
Arguments	Multiple date type arguments.
Return type	Returns a date type value.
Example	SELECT GREATEST(to_date('12-01-2024','MM-DD-YYYY'), to_date('06-01-2024','MM-DD-YYYY'), to_date('06-01-2023','MM-DD-YYYY')) AS later_date from dual;
Output	LATER_DATE --------- 01-DEC-24
Output	RDBMS

Aggregate Functions with Operators

Aggregate functions in SQL perform calculations on a group of values and return a single summarizing value.

They are primarily used with the GROUP BY clause but can also work on an entire dataset.

Aggregate functions like SUM(), COUNT(), AVG(), MAX(), and MIN() are often combined with other operators.

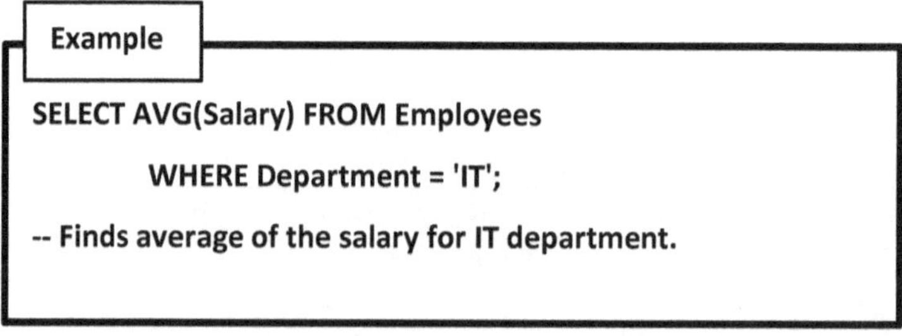

```sql
SELECT MAX(salary) AS MinimumSalary FROM employees;

-- Returns the highest value in a column.


SELECT COUNT(*) FROM Orders WHERE Status = 'Delivered';

-- Finds total count of orders which are delivered.


SELECT SUM(salary) AS TotalSalaries FROM employees;

-- Calculate the total salaries of employees.


SELECT MIN(salary) AS MinimumSalary FROM employees;

-- Returns the smallest value in a column.
```

GROUP BY, ORDER BY, and HAVING Clauses

These SQL clauses are essential for organizing, sorting, and filtering aggregated data in queries.

Group by clause

The GROUP BY clause groups rows that have the same values in specified columns into summary rows.

If a column have multiple rows with same value, we can make a group of that all rows. E.g. In employee's table department column may have same value for different employees (rows / records)

We can make group on department column, later we can perform different operations on that group E.g. we can find out average salary of specific department, we can count number of employees in a specific department.

Syntax

```
SELECT column1, column2, aggregate_function(column3)

    FROM table_name

    GROUP BY column1, column2;
```

Example

```
SELECT department, SUM(salary) AS TotalSalary

    FROM employees

    GROUP BY department;
```

Output

```
DEPARTMENT                                      TOTALSALARY

----------------------------------------------- -----------

Sales                                           145000

Marketing                                       133000

IT                                              180000

Finance                                         230000

Human Resources                                 158000
```

The ORDER BY clause is used to sort the result set in ascending (ASC) or descending (DESC) order.

By default, sorting is in ascending order. We can sort by one or more columns or expressions.

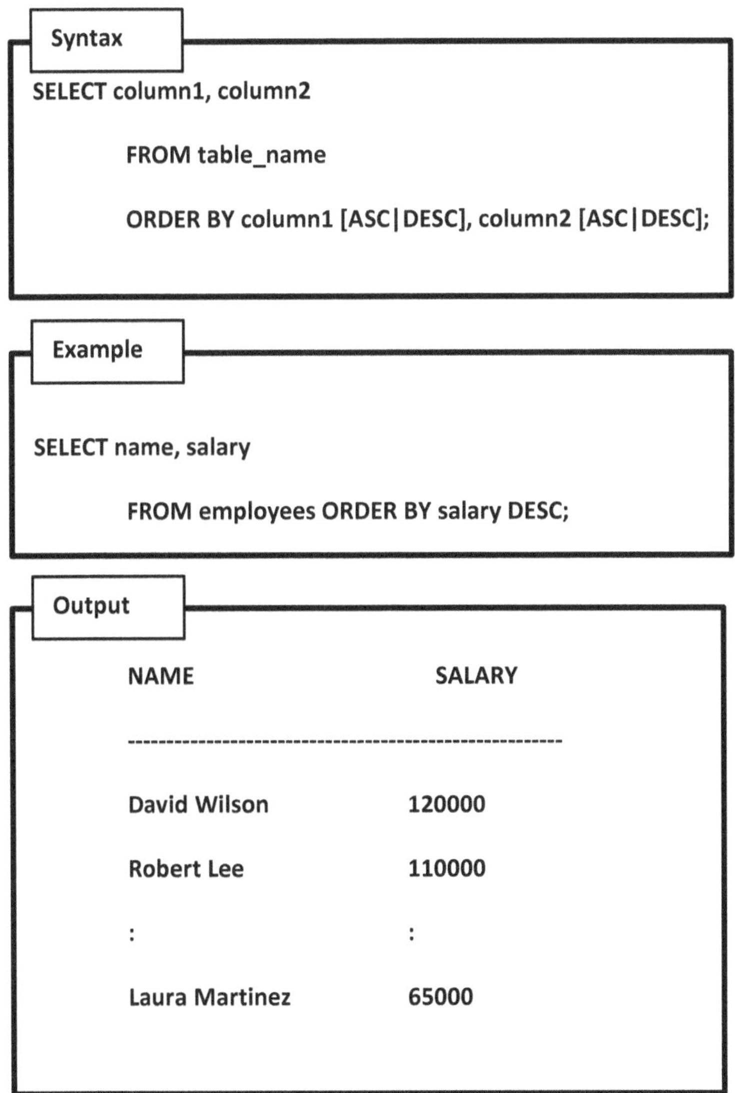

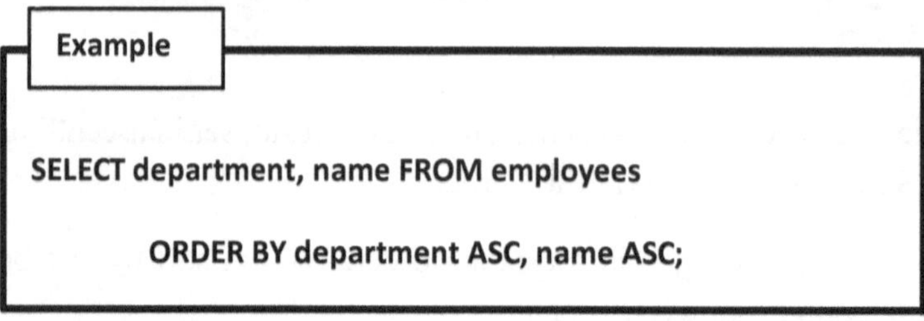

Example

```
SELECT department, name FROM employees

ORDER BY department ASC, name ASC;
```

Output

```
DEPARTMENT                          NAME

-----------------------------------------------------------------

Finance                             David Wilson

Finance                             Robert Lee

Human Resources                     Emily Davis

Human Resources                     Sophia White

IT                                  James Anderson

IT                                  Michael Brown

Marketing                           Laura Martinez

Marketing                           Sarah Johnson

Sales                               John Smith

Sales                               Olivia Garcia
```

In above example data set is sorted in ascending order as per department and then for every department, data is sorted in descending order as per name of employee.

Having clause

Consider a query "Display department names having total salary greater than 150000".

To get above required data we need to use sum() aggregate function to find out total salary paid

SELECT sum(salary) from employees;

Now we need to make a group of department to show "total salary department wise".

SELECT sum(salary) from employees group by department;

Now we have to compare total salary amount with 150000, since total salary amount is a **grouped data** (we are not able to use where clause), to compare it with a value 150000, we need **having** clause.

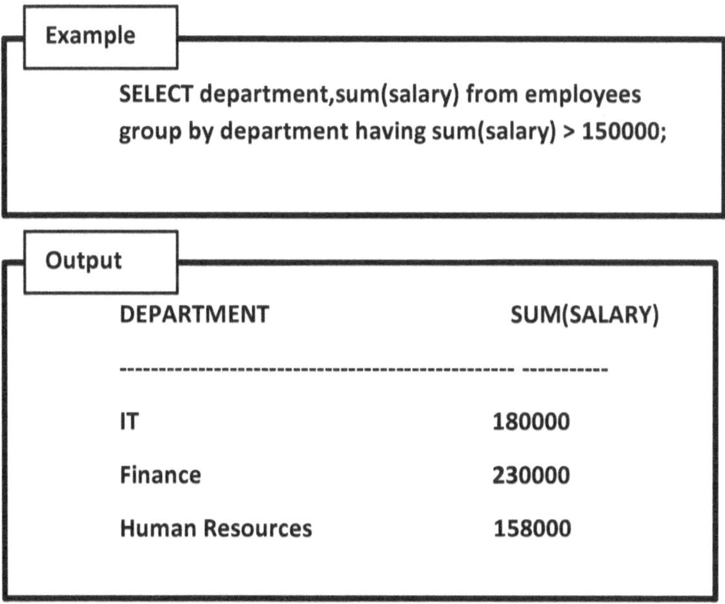

Now consider a query as follows

"Display department names in descending order of total salary having total salary greater than 150000 "

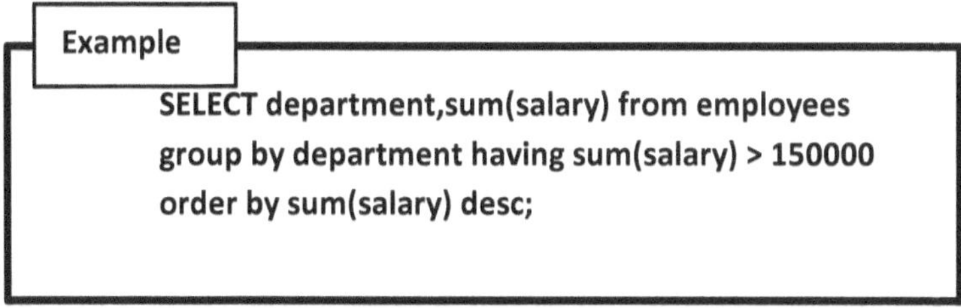

Views

o   Views are virtual tables OR part of tables.

o   A database relation may have large number of columns among the all columns some columns may consist crucial and important data that must be hidden from an end user.

o   For example, consider Salary of employee it contains financial information that may be confidential.

o   More than one views can be created for one table, to serve data to different users as per their requirement and access limit.

o   Views are just like database tables; we can insert, update and delete data. The changes done by DML commands in views are reflected in main table as well.

o   Therefore, we can conclude that there is no separate copy created in database for view, only the definition of view is stored in database.

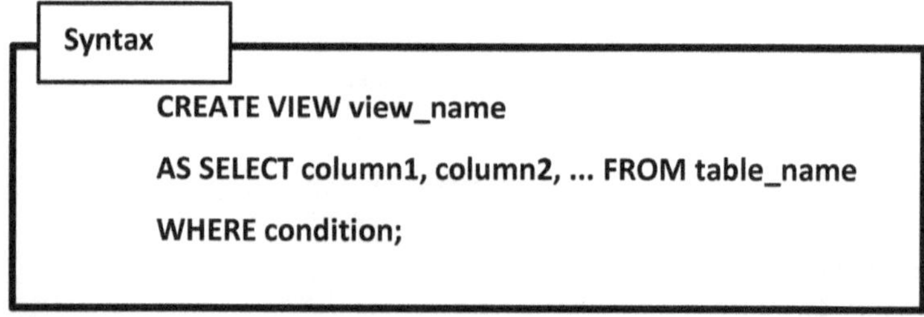

view_name: The name of the view you want to create.

SELECT statement: The query that defines the content of the view.

WHERE condition: Optional filtering criteria to limit the data in the view.

Now consider existing table employees with following schema, which have total six columns.

employees (e_id, name, joindate, salary, department, age, city)

We want to show information of employee to any end user, so one way is to grant him/her access on employees table, but here the problem is that, end user can see all columns data, now we want to hide joindate and salary data from end user. This is done by a database concept view, known as view level abstraction.

Consider following SQL command as an example.

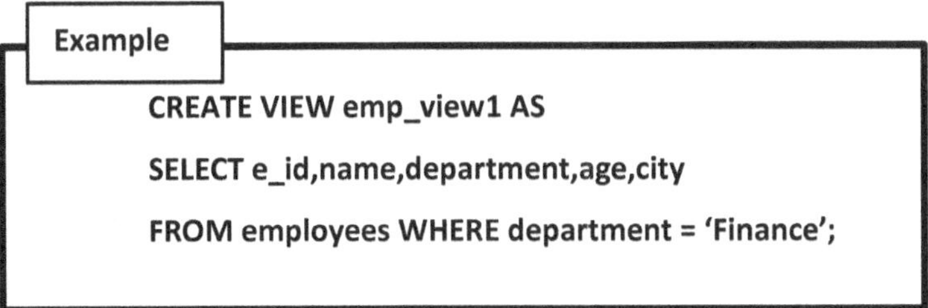

Now run a command

Select *from emp_view1;

Output

E_ID	NAME	DEPARTMENT	AGE	CITY
6005	David Wilson	Finance	50	Phoenix
6009	Robert Lee	Finance	45	Seattle

Insert operation on view

Observe the data of view emp_view1 as well as main table employees after executing insert command.

insert into emp_view1 values

(6011, 'Aman Verma', 'Finance', 34, 'Delhi');

Now display data of both emp_view1 and employees.

select *from emp_view1;

Output				
E_ID	**NAME**	**DEPARTMENT**	**AGE**	**CITY**
6005	**David Wilson**	**Finance**	**50**	**Phoenix**
6009	**Robert Lee**	**Finance**	**45**	**Seattle**
6010	**Aman Verma**	**Finance**	**34**	**Delhi**

select *from employees;

Out for above command will be

e_id	Name	Join Date	Salary	Department	Age	City
6001	John Smith	10-05-2017	75000	Sales	35	New York
6002	Sarah Johnson	21-08-2019	68000	Marketing	28	Los Angeles
6003	Michael Brown	15-03-2015	95000	IT	42	Chicago
6004	Emily Davis	04-11-2020	80000	Human Resources	31	Houston
6005	David Wilson	30-06-2013	120000	Finance	50	Phoenix
6006	Laura Martinez	12-09-2021	65000	Marketing	26	San Francisco
6007	James Anderson	18-04-2016	85000	IT	38	Dallas

6008	Olivia Garcia	10-01-2022	70000	Sales	29	Miami
6009	Robert Lee	22-07-2014	110000	Finance	45	Seattle
6010	Sophia White	28-02-2018	78000	Human Resources	33	Boston
6011	Aman Verma			Finance	34	Delhi

Snapshot

- Snapshot is a database object which is use to save database (table) state at a point of time.

- Snapshot also known as Materialized View OR Static View.

- Any DML command cannot be permitted on snapshot. (unlike view)

- Separate copy maintained in database. (unlike view)

- Any manipulation in database main table not reflected in snapshot. (unlike view)

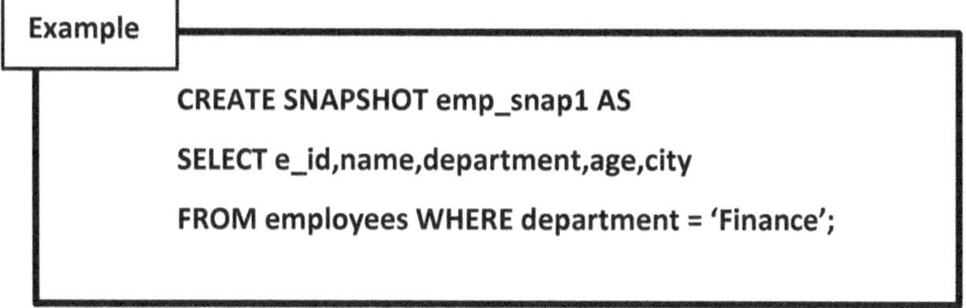

Synonym

- Synonyms provide alternate name to the database object such as table, view.

- o Synonyms permit applications to function without modification regardless of which user owns the table or view and regardless of which database holds the table or view.

- o However, synonyms are not a substitute for privileges on database objects. Appropriate privileges must be granted to a user before the user can use the synonym.

- o There are two major uses of synonyms:

  - Object invisibility: Synonyms can be created to keep the original object hidden from the user.

  - Location invisibility: Synonyms can be created as aliases for tables and other objects that are not part of the local database.

- o There are two types of synonym as follows

  - Public Synonym. (another user can directly access)

  - Private Synonym. (another user cannot directly access without a location hierarchy)

<table>
<tr><td>Synatx</td></tr>
<tr><td>

Private synonym

     CREATE SYNONYM SynonymName FOR tableName;

Public Synonym

     CREATE PUBLIC SYNONYM SynonymName FOR tableName;= 'Finance';

</td></tr>
</table>

Private synonym

CREATE SYNONYM emp FOR employees;

Public Synonym

CREATE PUBLIC SYNONYM emp_pub FOR employees;

Sequence

- o A Sequence is a database object that generates unique integer numbers in sequential order.

- o Sequences are used to generate primary key values or unique key values automatically either in ascending or descending order.

- o Some DBMS like MySQL supports AUTO_INCREMENT in place of Sequence. AUTO_INCREMENT is applied on columns, it automatically increments the column value by 1 each time a new record is entered into the table.

- o Sequence is also somewhat similar to AUTO_INCREMENT but its has some extra features in Oracle.

Parameters to create sequence

Initial-value →	It specifies the starting value of the Sequence,
Increment-value →	It is the value by which sequence will be incremented
maxvalue →	It specifies the maximum value until which sequence will increment itself.

cycle →   It specifies that if the maximum value exceeds
                           the set limit, sequence will restart its cycle from
                           the beginning.

No cycle →   It specifies that if sequence exceeds maxvalue an
                           error will be thrown.

Sequence has two pointer variables

NEXTVAL

- o Retrieves the next value in the sequence and increments the
    sequence.

- o You call NEXTVAL to generate a new, unique value from a
    sequence.

CURRVAL

- o Retrieves the current value of the sequence for the current
    session (the last value generated by NEXTVAL).

- o CURRVAL can only be called after NEXTVAL has been
    invoked in the same session. It does not increment the sequence.

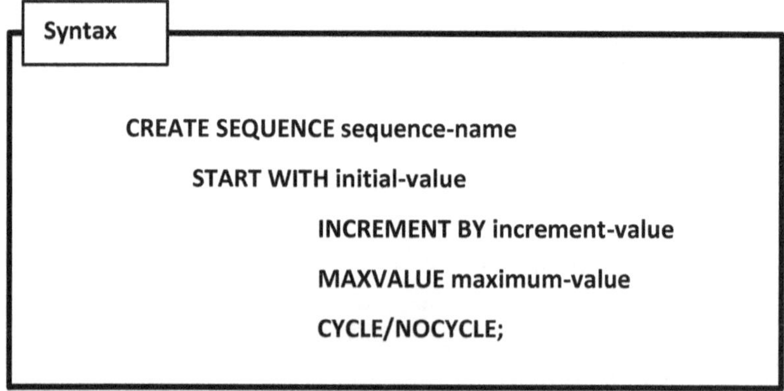

```
Example

    CREATE SEQUENCE reg_id_seq
        START WITH 1
            INCREMENT BY 1
            MAXVALUE 100
            NOCYCLE ;
```

We have created a sequence database object, but the question arise how and where I can use it. To understand use of sequence database object, let's create one table as following schema.

registration(reg_id, participant_name, event_name, college_name);

Above table is to store data of participants, those registering for an event. The organizing committee decided that we allow only 100 registration.

They designed Web Application form to accept data from students of various colleges.

Students are entering their name, event name and their college name, but they are not entering value for field reg_id.

As a web application programmer, we are going to design registration table in such a way that reg_id value must be taken from reg_id_seq sequence, for that we will use the insert command as follows.

insert into registration values

(reg_id_nextval, 'Arpit', 'Quiz Contest', 'AIARKP');

We can observe that reg_id column value coming from sequence database object.

Since sequence max value is 100, it will provide only 100 registrations.

Index

An index in a database is a data structure that improves the speed of data retrieval operations on a table. It is similar to an index in a book, which allows you to locate information quickly without scanning the entire content.

Advantages

- o Improved Query Performance:

    Indexes allow the database to find rows faster, especially for large datasets.

- o Efficient Sorting:

    Indexes enable faster sorting of data.

- o Enforced Uniqueness:

    Unique indexes ensure no duplicate values exist in a column.

- o Quick Searches:

    Speeds up operations like SELECT, JOIN, and WHERE queries.

Types of Indexes

Primary Index

- o Automatically created when a table has a primary key.
- o Ensures the uniqueness of rows in the table.

Unique Index

- o Ensures all values in the indexed column(s) are unique.
- o Created manually for non-primary key columns.

Example

CREATE UNIQUE INDEX idx_unique_email ON Users(Email);

Composite Index

- o   An index created on multiple columns.

Example

CREATE INDEX idx_composite ON Orders(CustomerID, OrderDate);

Joins

A join in a database is used to combine rows from two or more tables based on a related column between them. Joins enable queries to fetch data distributed across multiple tables in a relational database. Different types of joins are as follows

1. Inner Join
2. Left Join (or Left Outer Join)
3. Right Join (or Right Outer Join)
4. Full Join (or Full Outer Join)
5. Cross Join
6. Self Join

CustomerID	Name	City
1	Alice	New York
2	Bob	Los Angeles
3	Charlie	Chicago

Table: Customers

OrderID	CustomerID	Product	Amount
101	1	Laptop	1200
102	2	Smartphone	800
103	1	Headphone	200
104	4	Tablet	500

Table: Orders

Create above two tables to understand implementation of databse joins.

Inner join

An inner join returns only the rows where there is a match in common column values of both tables.

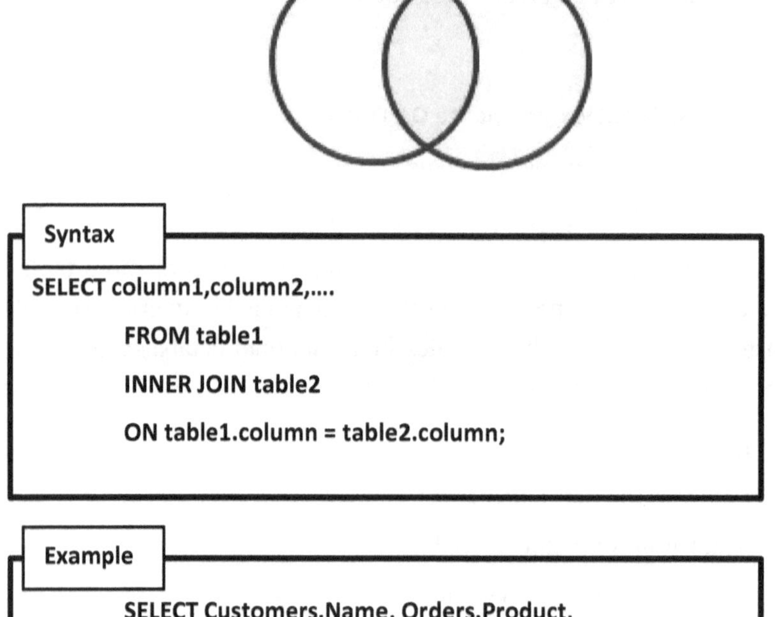

Syntax

SELECT column1,column2,....

    FROM table1

    INNER JOIN table2

    ON table1.column = table2.column;

Example

    SELECT Customers.Name, Orders.Product, Orders.Amount

    FROM Customers

    INNER JOIN Orders

    ON Customers.Customer_ID = Orders.Customer_ID;

Observe the table on next page, the shaded records are the the records which will be displayed as resultant table.

Customers			Orders			
CustomerID	Name	City	OrderID	CustomerID	Product	Amount
1	Alice	New York	101	1	Laptop	1200
1	Alice	New York	102	2	Smartphone	800
1	Alice	New York	103	1	Headphone	200
1	Alice	New York	104	4	Tablet	500
2	Bob	Los Angeles	101	1	Laptop	1200
2	Bob	Los Angeles	102	2	Smartphone	800
2	Bob	Los Angeles	103	1	Headphone	200
2	Bob	Los Angeles	104	4	Tablet	500
3	Charlie	Chicago	101	1	Laptop	1200
3	Charlie	Chicago	102	2	Smartphone	800
3	Charlie	Chicago	103	1	Headphone	200
3	Charlie	Chicago	104	4	Tablet	500

Result of inner join of customers and orders relation is records with common customer id's as highlighted in above table.

Therefore, the output will be as follows

Output

CUSTOMER_ID	NAME	CITY	ORDER_ID	CUSTOMER_ID	PRODUCT	AMOUNT
1	Alice	New York	101	1	Laptop	1200
2	Bob	Los Angeles	102	2	Smartphone	800
1	Alice	New York	103	1	Headphone	200

Left join

LEFT JOIN fetch all the rows of the table on the left side of the join and matches rows for the table on the right side of the join. For the rows for which there is no matching row on the right side, the result-set will contain null. LEFT JOIN is also known as LEFT OUTER JOIN.

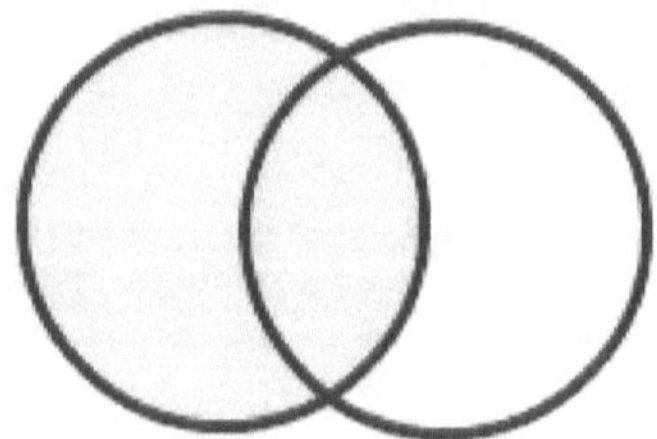

Syntax

```
SELECT column1,colum2,....

FROM table1

LEFT JOIN table2

ON table1.column = table2.column;
```

Example

```
SELECT Customers.Name, Orders.Product,
Orders.Amount

FROM Customers

LEFT JOIN Orders

ON Customers.Customer_ID = Orders.Customer_ID;
```

Output

CUSTOMER_ID	NAME	CITY	ORDER_ID	CUSTOMER_ID	PRODUCT	AMOUNT
1	Alice	New York	101	1	Laptop	1200
2	Bob	Los Angeles	102	2	Smartphone	800
1	Alice	New York	103	1	Headphone	200
3	Charlie	Chicago				

Righ join

Right Join returns all the rows of the table on the right side of the join and matching rows for the table on the left side of the join. It is very similar to Left Join for the rows for which there is no matching row on the left side, the result-set will contain null. Right Join is also known as Right Outer Join.

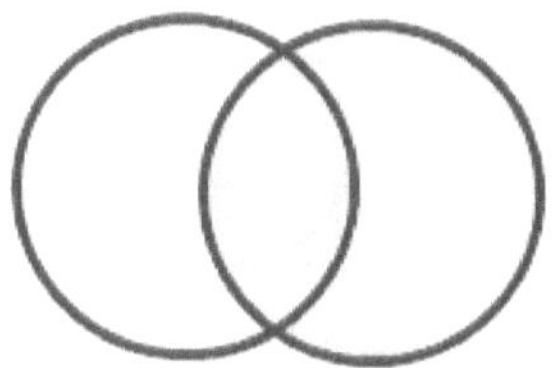

Syntax

SELECT column1,colum2,….

FROM table1

RIGHT JOIN table2

ON table1.column = table2.column;

Example

SELECT Customers.Name, Orders.Product, Orders.Amount

FROM Customers

RIGHT JOIN Orders

ON Customers.Customer_ID = Orders.Customer_ID;

Output

CUSTOMER_ID	NAME	CITY	ORDER_ID	CUSTOMER_ID	PRODUCT	AMOUNT
1	Alice	New York	101	1	Laptop	1200
2	Bob	Los Angeles	102	2	Smartphone	800
1	Alice	New York	103	1	Headphone	200
			104	4	Tablet	500

Full join

Full Join creates the result-set by combining results of both Left Join and Right Join. The result-set will contain all the rows from both tables. For the rows for which there is no matching, the result-set will contain NULL values.

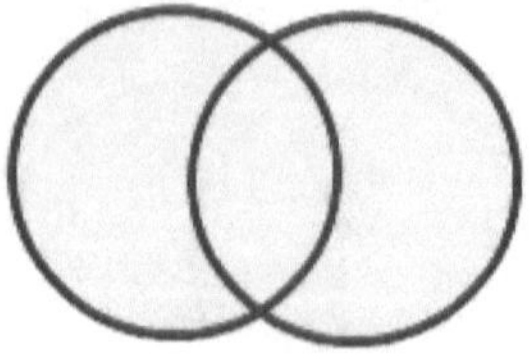

<table>
<tr><td>Syntax</td></tr>
</table>

```
SELECT column1,colum2,....

FROM table1

FULL OUTER JOIN table2

ON table1.column = table2.column;
```

<table>
<tr><td>Example</td></tr>
</table>

```
SELECT Customers.Name, Orders.Product,
Orders.Amount

FROM Customers

FULL OUTER JOIN Orders

ON Customers.Customer_ID = Orders.Customer_ID;
```

Output

CUSTOMER_ID	NAME	CITY	ORDER_ID	CUSTOMER_ID	PRODUCT	AMOUNT
1	Alice	New York	101	1	Laptop	1200
2	Bob	Los Angeles	102	2	Smartphone	800
1	Alice	New York	103	1	Headphone	200
			104	4	Tablet	500
3	Charlie	Chicago				

Cross join

Fetch all records from both tables. Include records with no matches in either table, showing NULL for unmatched data.

Syntax

```
SELECT column1,colum2,....

FROM table1

CROSS JOIN table2 ;
```

Syntax

```
SELECT column1,colum2,....

FROM table1 , table2 ;
```

Example

```
SELECT *FROM Customers CROSS JOIN Orders ;

OR

SELECT *FROM Customers , Orders ;
```

Output

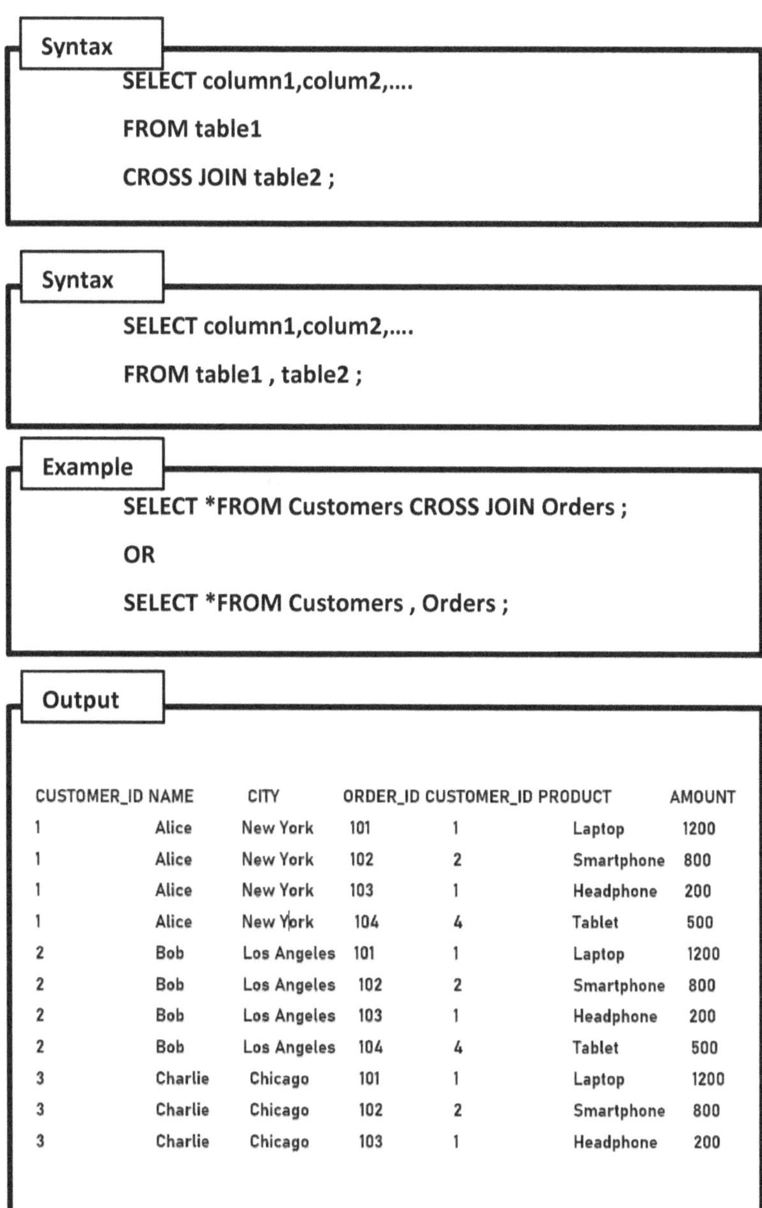

CUSTOMER_ID	NAME	CITY	ORDER_ID	CUSTOMER_ID	PRODUCT	AMOUNT
1	Alice	New York	101	1	Laptop	1200
1	Alice	New York	102	2	Smartphone	800
1	Alice	New York	103	1	Headphone	200
1	Alice	New York	104	4	Tablet	500
2	Bob	Los Angeles	101	1	Laptop	1200
2	Bob	Los Angeles	102	2	Smartphone	800
2	Bob	Los Angeles	103	1	Headphone	200
2	Bob	Los Angeles	104	4	Tablet	500
3	Charlie	Chicago	101	1	Laptop	1200
3	Charlie	Chicago	102	2	Smartphone	800
3	Charlie	Chicago	103	1	Headphone	200

6. Transaction Management

Transaction

Collections of database operations that form a *single logical unit of work* are called transactions. Transaction must be written in such a way that, they do not violate any database-consistency constraints. Means that if the database was consistent at the start of transaction, the database must be consistent when the transaction successfully ends.

A transaction is a unit of program execution that accesses and possibly updates various data items. Usually, a transaction is initiated by a user program written in a high-level data-manipulation language or programming language.

Transaction T1 (To deposit 30000 amount from account A to

[At the start: Database State: Total balance = 90000

Balance (A) = 50000

Balance (B) = 40000]

1. Start the transaction using **START TRANSACTION**; to ensure all steps are executed together.
2. Deduct 30,000 from Account A using an **UPDATE** statement.
3. Add 30,000 to Account B using another **UPDATE** statement.
4. Check the balance of Account A to prevent overdraft.
5. If sufficient funds exist, **COMMIT** the transaction (confirm changes).
6. If not, **ROLLBACK** to undo all changes and prevent an invalid transfer.
7. Provide a success or failure message for confirmation.

[At the End: Database State: Total balance = 90000

Balance (A) = 20000

Balance (B) = 70000]

For maintaining *data integrity* and *reliability* in databases, especially for transactions like money transfers, banking, e-commerce, and booking systems, Transactions must maintain some properties; these properties are known as ACID properties.

ACID properties

In database systems, ACID properties ensure that transactions are reliable, consistent, and fault-tolerant. These properties are essential for data integrity and error-free transaction processing, especially in critical applications like banking, e-commerce, and reservation systems.

Atomicity

Either all operations of the transaction are reflected properly in the database, or none are.

Consistency

Execution of a transaction in isolation (that is, with no other transaction executing concurrently) preserves the consistency of the database.

Isolation

Even though multiple transactions may execute concurrently, the system guarantees that, for every pair of transactions Ti and Tj , it appears to Ti that either Tj finished execution before Ti started, or Tj started execution after Ti finished. Thus, each transaction is unaware of other transactions executing concurrently in the system.

Durability

After a transaction completes successfully, the changes it has made to the database persist, even if there are system failures.

In Transacrtion management, at a time not a single transaction is in execution but may be multiple transactions are in execution. In such cases it is mandatory to maintain database in consistent state.

To full fill this requirement a concept that is used is nothing but *schedule*.

Schedule

In Transaction Management, a schedule is a sequence of operations (such as read, write, commit, and abort) performed by multiple transactions in a database system. Schedules play a crucial role in ensuring concurrency control and maintaining the ACID properties of transactions.

A well-designed schedule ensures that transactions execute efficiently and correctly, preventing issues like data inconsistency, lost updates, and deadlocks.

Schedules can be classified into different types based on their *execution order* and the level of concurrency control applied.

Serial Schedules

> Serial schedules are the schedules in which after successful completion one transaction (all steps/instructions completed) only another transaction execution is starts. (Refer figure 2.2)

Concurrent Schedules

> A concurrent schedule is a schedule in which two transactions are running concurrently (on same time), means the operating system may execute some steps/instructions of one transaction for a little while, then switch to another transaction and execute the second transaction for some time, and then switch back to the first transaction for some time, and so on. (Refer figure 2.3)

Consider following transactions.

Transaction-1: Transferring Rs.5000 amount from account A to account B.

Transaction-2: Transferring 20% of account A's balance to account B.

Transaction-1	Transaction-2

	read($A_{balance}$);
	amount := (($A_{balance}$*20)/100)
	$A_{balance}$:= $A_{balance}$ − amount;
	write($A_{balance}$);
	read($B_{balance}$);
	$B_{balance}$:= $B_{balance}$ + amount;
	write($B_{balance}$);
	commit;

read($A_{balance}$);
$A_{balance}$:= $A_{balance}$ − 5000;
write($A_{balance}$);
read($B_{balance}$);
$B_{balance}$:= $B_{balance}$ + 5000;
write($B_{balance}$);
commit;	

Fig. 6.1 Serial Schedule

Transaction-1	Transaction-2

read($A_{balance}$);
$A_{balance}$:= $A_{balance}$ − 5000;
write($A_{balance}$);	

	read($A_{balance}$);
	amount := (($A_{balance}$*20)/100)
	$A_{balance}$:= $A_{balance}$ − amount;
	write($A_{balance}$);

read($B_{balance}$);
$B_{balance}$:= $B_{balance}$ + 5000;
write($B_{balance}$);
commit;	

	read($B_{balance}$);
	$B_{balance}$:= $B_{balance}$ + amount;
	write($B_{balance}$);
	commit

Fig. 6.2 Concurrent Schedule

Problem with Concurrent Schedule

Concurrent schedules may result in an inconsistence state. To understand it, consider the concurrent schedule of Figure 6.3 (Consider $A_{balance}$ initially is 10000 and $B_{balance}$ initially is 20000).

At the start of execution of transactions 30000 is the overall amount.

Transaction-1		Transaction-2	
read($A_{balance}$); $A_{balance} := A_{balance} - 500$;	$A_{balance}=10000$ $A_{balance}=9500$		

		read($A_{balance}$);
		amount $:= ((A_{balance}*20)/100)$
		$A_{balance} := A_{balance} - $ amount;
		write($A_{balance}$);
		read($B_{balance}$);
			$A_{balance}=10000$
			amount=1000
			$A_{balance}=9000$
			$A_{balance}=9000$
			$B_{balance}=20000$

write($A_{balance}$);
read($B_{balance}$);
$B_{balance} := B_{balance} + 500$;
write($B_{balance}$);
commit;
	$A_{balance}=9500$
	$B_{balance}=20000$
	$B_{balance}=20500$
	$B_{balance}=20500$		

		$B_{balance} := B_{balance} + $ amount; write($B_{balance}$); commit	$B_{balance}=21000$ $B_{balance}=21000$

Fig. 6.3 Concurrent Schedule

After execution of transaction 1 and 2 as per above schedule, the final database state is an inconsistent state, because finally $A_{balance}=9500$ and $B_{balance}=21000$, overall amount is 30500, however at the start of transactions database state with overall amount was 30000. [500 extra amount is saved].

To avoid such an inconsistency in database, we need a concurrent schedule who act as a serial schedule.

Serializability

Serializable schedule

"A concurrent schedule after execution has the effect same as a serial schedule on database state is known as serializable schedule."

> *Serializability* ensures that a non-serial schedule (where multiple transactions execute concurrently) is equivalent to a serial schedule (where transactions execute one after another). This prevents issues like lost updates, dirty reads, and uncommitted dependencies while allowing concurrency.

In Transaction Management, a serializable schedule ensures that concurrent transactions produce the same result as if they were executed one after another (serially). It is the strongest form of schedule correctness and guarantees data consistency and integrity.

If two transactions (T1 and T2) modify the same account balance, serializability ensures that their execution does not cause incorrect results.

A serializable schedule ensures that the database remains in a consistent state before and after transaction execution.

It prevents issues like lost updates, dirty reads, and uncommitted dependencies.

Serializable schedule maintains isolation in Concurrent Transactions.

A serializable schedule allows multiple transactions to execute simultaneously, while ensuring the final outcome is the same as a serial execution.

There are two main types of serializability:

1. View Serializability

2. Conflict Serializability

View Serializability

A schedule is view-serializable if it produces the same final result as a serial schedule, even if it cannot be transformed by swapping non-conflicting operations.

Now lets explore conflict serializability in detail.

Conflict Serializability

Conflict Serializability is a condition in which a non-serial schedule of transactions can be transformed into a serial schedule by swapping non-conflicting operations while maintaining the same final outcome. It ensures that concurrent transactions execute in a way that preserves database consistency.

Two operations in different transactions conflict if:

o   They operate on the same data item.

o   At least one of them is a WRITE operation.

Example

Operation 1	Operation 2	Same Data Item?	Conflict?
Read (A) in T1	Read (A) in T2	Yes	No Conflict
Read (A) in T1	Write (A) in T2	Yes	Conflict
Write (A) in T1	Read (A) in T2	Yes	Conflict
Write (A) in T1	Write (A) in T2	Yes	Conflict

Testing of Conflict Serializability

Steps to check conflict Serializability

1. Identify conflicting operations between transactions.

2. Construct a precedence graph (also called a wait-for graph).

3. If there are no cycles in the graph, the schedule is conflict-serializable.

4. If a cycle exists, the schedule is not conflict-serializable.

Example 1:

Now consider following schedule with two transactions T1 and T2 operating on data items A and B.

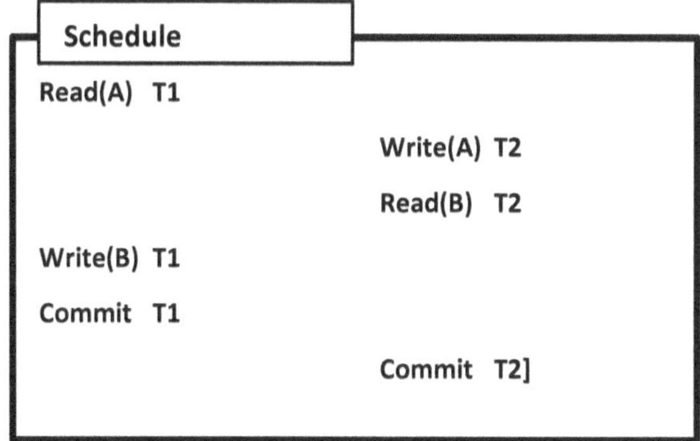

Step 1: Identify Conflicting Operations

Read(A) in T1 → Write(A) in T2 → Conflict (T1 → T2)

Read(B) in T2 → Write(B) in T1 → Conflict (T2 → T1)

Step 2: Construct the Precedence Graph

A cycle (T1 → T2 → T1) is present, meaning the schedule is not conflict-serializable.

Example 2:

Now consider following schedule with two transactions T1 and T2 operating on data items A and B.

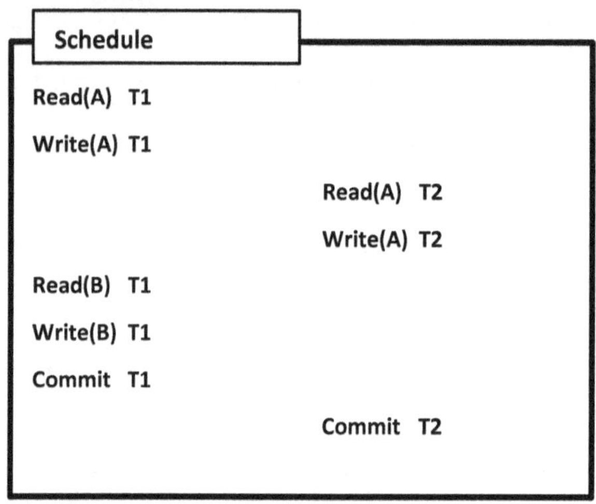

Step 1: Identify Conflicting Operations

Read(A) in T1 → Write(A) in T2 → Conflict (T1 → T2)

Write(A) in T1 → Read(A) in T2 → Conflict (T1 → T2)

Write(A) in T1 → Write(A) in T2 → Conflict (T1 → T2)

Write(B) in T1 → Write(B) in T2 → Conflict (T1 → T2)

Step 2: Construct the Precedence Graph

A cycle is not present, meaning the schedule is conflict-serializable.

Concurrency Control

Concurrency control is a mechanism used in database management systems (DBMS) to ensure that multiple transactions can execute simultaneously without causing inconsistencies, lost updates, or data corruption.

In a multi-user environment, multiple transactions may try to access and modify the same data at the same time, leading to problems such as:

o   Reading uncommitted data from another transaction.

o   One transaction overwrites another's update.

o   A value changes between reads of the same transaction.

To prevent these issues, concurrency control techniques are used.

Concurrency Control Techniques

Concurrency control methods ensure that transactions execute in a way that preserves database consistency while allowing parallel execution. The main techniques are:

Lock-Based Recovery Technique

Lock-based recovery techniques in Database Management Systems (DBMS) ensure that transactions execute safely and the database remains consistent even in the event of failures. By using locks with logging and rollback mechanisms, the system prevents data corruption, lost updates, and cascading rollbacks.

Locking Protocols

o   Two-Phase Locking (2PL)

o   Strict Two-Phase Locking (Strict 2PL)

Types of Locks

- Shared Lock

  - Allows multiple transactions to read a data item but prevents writing.

- Exclusive Lock

  - Allows only one transaction to read and write a data item.

  - Prevents other transactions from accessing the data until the lock is released.

Timestamp-Based Protocols

Each transaction is assigned a timestamp (TS) when it starts. Transactions execute based on their timestamps to maintain serializability.

Rules:

- If an older transaction wants to write after a newer transaction has read, it is aborted.

- If a newer transaction wants to write before an older transaction has read, it is aborted.

Two-Phase Locking (2PL)

Two-Phase Locking (2PL) is a concurrency control protocol that ensures serializability in transactions by dividing the execution of a transaction into two distinct phases:

Growing Phase – The transaction acquires all the necessary locks.

Shrinking Phase – The transaction releases locks but cannot acquire new ones.

This mechanism prevents conflicts and ensures consistency in concurrent transactions.

Phases of Two-Phase Locking (2PL)

1. Growing Phase

    o   A transaction can acquire locks (Shared (S) or Exclusive (X) locks) on data items.

    o   However, it cannot release any locks in this phase.

    o   The transaction continues acquiring locks until it reaches the Lock Point (LP), where it gets all the locks it needs.

2. Shrinking Phase

    o   Once the transaction releases its first lock, it enters the shrinking phase.

    o   In this phase, it can only release locks but cannot acquire new locks.

    o   The transaction continues until it commits or aborts.

Example of Two-Phase Locking (2PL)

Consider two transactions T1 and T2, both accessing data items A and B.

Growing Phase:

    o   T1 acquires locks on A and B before unlocking any locks.

Shrinking Phase:

    o   Once T1 releases A, it does not acquire any new locks.

    o   Similarly, T2 also follows the two-phase rule.

The schedule is serializable because T1 executes before T2.

Step	Transaction T1	Transaction T2
1	Lock(A)	
2	Read(A)	
3	Lock(B)	
4	Read(B)	
5	Unlock(A) (Shrinking Phase starts)	
6	Write(B)	
7	Unlock(B)	
8	Commit	
9		Lock(A) (Now T2 starts)
10		Read(A)
11		Lock(B)
12		Read(B)
13		Unlock(A) (Shrinking Phase starts)
14		Write(B)
15		Unlock(B)
16		Commit

Strict Two-Phase Locking (Strict 2PL)

Strict Two-Phase Locking (Strict 2PL) is an enhanced version of Two-Phase Locking (2PL) that ensures stronger isolation in database transactions. It prevents cascading rollbacks by holding all exclusive (X) locks until the transaction commits or aborts.

Rules of Strict 2PL

- o A transaction acquires locks during execution (Growing Phase).

- o A transaction does not release any exclusive locks (X-Locks) until commit or abort.

- o Shared locks (S-Locks) may be released before commit, but X-Locks remain locked until the transaction finishes.

Example of Strict 2PL

Consider two transactions T1 and T2, both accessing data items A and B.

Step	Transaction T1	Transaction T2	Locks Held
1	Lock(A) (X)		A (T1 - X)
2	Read(A)		A (T1 - X)
3	Write(A)		A (T1 - X)
4	Lock(B) (X)		A (T1 - X), B (T1 - X)
5	Read(B)		A (T1 - X), B (T1 - X)
6	Write(B)		A (T1 - X), B (T1 - X)
7	Commit T1		Now releases A & B
8		Lock(A) (X)	A (T2 - X)

9		Read(A)	A (T2 - X)
10		Write(A)	A (T2 - X)
11		Commit T2	Now releases A

- T1 holds locks on A and B until commit.

- T2 cannot acquire locks on A or B until T1 commits.

- Prevents cascading rollbacks, ensuring data consistency.

Deadlock

A deadlock in a database occurs when two or more transactions are waiting for resources held by each other, creating a cycle of dependency that prevents any of them from proceeding. This situation leads to indefinite waiting unless the deadlock is detected and resolved.

Transaction T1 sets an exclusive lock on object A, T2 sets an exclusive lock on B, T1 requests an exclusive lock on B and is queued, and T2 requests an exclusive lock on A and is queued. Now, T1 is waiting for T2 to release its lock and T2 is waiting for T1 to release its lock.

Such a cycle of transactions waiting for locks to be released is called a deadlock.

Deadlock Prevention Technique

Timeouts –

If a transaction waits too long, it is aborted.

Lock Ordering –

Transactions acquire locks in a predefined order to avoid circular wait conditions.

Deadlock Detection –

The system periodically checks for deadlocks and resolves them by rolling back one or more transactions.

Wait-Die and Wound-Wait Schemes –

These prioritize older transactions over newer ones to avoid deadlocks.

Wait-Die Scheme

If an transaction (T1) requests a resource held by a younger transaction (T2), T1 waits.

If a younger transaction (T2) requests a resource held by an older transaction (T1), T2 is aborted (dies) and restarted later.

Example:

- o T1 (older) requests a resource held by T2 (younger) → T1 waits.

- o T2 (younger) requests a resource held by T1 (older) → T2 is aborted (dies).

Wound-Wait Scheme

If an older transaction (T1) requests a resource held by a younger transaction (T2), T2 is aborted (wounded) and restarted later.

If a younger transaction (T2) requests a resource held by an older transaction (T1), T2 waits.

Example:

- o T1 (older) requests a resource held by T2 (younger) → T2 is aborted (wounded).

- o T2 (younger) requests a resource held by T1 (older) → T2 waits.